L-10-06

SCRAPBOOK STYLES

Fabrics & Florals

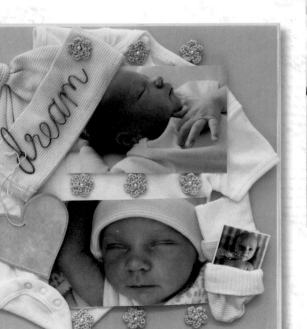

On April 11, 1942, Army Chaplain Captain Wertz united in holy matrimony

Harrietta Sims and 2nd Lt. Hal Randolph

at Camp Robinson Little Rock Arkansas

Grow old along with me! The best is yet to be, the last of life, for which the first was made.

Mrs Crona Schuller was the Matron of Honor and Lt. Raleigh was Best Man. He and Hal had been best friends since their college days at North Carolina State, thru ROTC and served in the US Army together.

RANDOLPH

dream

SCRAPBOOK STYLES

Fabrics & Florals

JILL MILLER

100+ IDEAS FOR
"DRESSING UP" YOUR PAGES!

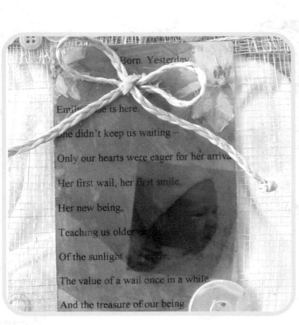

Watson-Guptill Publications / New York

Senior Acquisitions Editor: Joy Aquilino
Edited by Amy Handy
Designed by Georgia Rucker Design
Graphic production by Hector Campbell

First published in 2006 by Watson-Guptill Publications,
a division of VNU Business Media, Inc.,
770 Broadway, New York, NY 10003
www.wgpub.com

Library of Congress Control Number:
2005928139

ISBN 0-8230-1637-4

Printed in China

First printing, 2006

1 2 3 4 5 6 7 8 9 / 14 13 12 11 10 09 08 07 06

CONTENTS

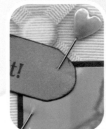

Introduction

All our lives, from the first moments after birth until the day we pass on, we are wrapped up in fabric. Indeed, many precious memories involve that special blanket or holiday dress or rock 'n' roll T-shirt or bridal gown. So it seems only natural that we should include fabric in our scrapbooks. Fabric accents and fabric papers are readily available, but do not forget to include sentimental pieces from your own wardrobe as well.

The scrapbook pages showcased in this book offer many ideas for incorporating fabric elements into your own scrapbooks. Most of the supplies are easily found at craft stores or online, and although a few of the specific store-bought items may not be available in your area, you should have no trouble finding a similar substitute—perhaps even a better one from your own closet or craft shelf.

A fair number of pages illustrate the use of florals as decorative accents. If you are lucky, Mother Nature has surrounded you with flowers of all varieties. Press them, then preserve them in your scrapbooks. If you don't have a bounty of beauty available, consider purchasing pressed florals or use silk imitations. You'll find many of them in the page layouts that follow.

While you may be familiar with the use of pressed flowers and natural twine or raffia for scrapbooking, you may not have seen pages with seaweed, woven grass mats, paper whites, ferns, and holly leaves. Silk versions of each of these items are used in this book. If you're already thinking, "But won't those items be harmful to my photographs?" don't worry. De-acidification products, shadowboxes, and extra-deep page protectors help to minimize the risks associated with using artificial, dimensional accents such as these. This book also includes paper, ribbon, and vellum flowers that are safe and easy to replicate yourself.

In addition to incorporating actual fabrics and floral accents, you will also find techniques for adding texture with fabric paints, printing on fabric sheets, and using quilting software on your computer, as well as how to add shimmer and shine with snaps, beads, fabric bags, and charms. Ribbons, threads, and stitched effects—already very popular and widely used—are shown here in new and unique applications.

Since fabric varies widely in texture, weight, and thickness, a quick overview of effective adhesives is important here. While liquid glues, especially fabric glues, work well for most crafting applications, they are not ideal for securing fabrics to paper. You can achieve good adhesion without the mess using aggressive dry adhesives such as glue dots or carpet tape. Nail heads, spiral clips, and brads secure fabrics and florals in place while also adding decorative details at the same time. Many of the pages that have an abundance of fabric stretching from end to end are actually secured with heavy-duty packaging tape on the back of the cardstock base. Always use cardstock when working with fabrics to help the page keep its shape. Mount text-weight specialty papers onto cardstock if necessary.

Natural fabrics are the safest to use when placed next to your photographs. If you can't find natural fabrics or wish to use a synthetic blend, be sure to mount your photos onto acid-free, archival cardstock mats to create a buffer between your photos and your fabrics. If the fabric overlaps a photo, spray it with de-acidification spray or else create your scrapbook page with a duplicate copy of the photo. It's also a good idea to spray any floral accents with a de-acidifying mist before adhering these items to your page.

Designing with fabrics and florals is one of the best ways to kick-start your creativity! Since these wonderful backgrounds and accents are often "good to go" right off the store shelves, you'll find that they add instant appeal to your pages. And because adding fabrics and florals to your scrapbooking pages may be a new approach for you, you'll find your mind filled with many possibilities, all the while feeling a sense of comfort and familiarity, because fabrics and florals have been a part of your life since the very beginning.

CHAPTER ONE

No-Sew Sheer Fabrics

Sheer fabrics lend instant shimmer and softness to any scrapbook page. The lightweight quality of the fabric makes it tricky to sew on a machine but it's perfect for mounting on paper with just a tuck here, a bit of glue there, and a gather or two everywhere. You can tape the fabric's raw edges on the back of your page or leave them exposed. Draped sheers, sheer fabric wraps, and sheer accents add a sense of warmth and luxury while leaving your sewing machine out in the cold. For the times when just a small touch of sheer is all that's needed to soften a page, subdue a too-strong visual element, or inject a bit of elegance, sheer ribbon is the perfect solution.

Draped Sheers

Tiebacks

Julie's long, flowing white wedding dress and her single strand of pearls are reflected perfectly in the white and soft pastel sheer fabrics (taped to the back of the page), pearl tiebacks, mini pearl accents (adhered with tiny glue dots), and small delicate roses. A premade white calligraphy bookplate balances the large framed photo, and a faux stitched rose has simply been ironed on to the sheer white panel to provide a subtle white-on-white finishing touch, which completes this beautiful page for a beautiful blushing bride.

Blushing Bride

Design: Jill Miller
Photography: Cary Oliver
INTERMEDIATE

Precut photo frame, strung pearls: Michaels
Harlequin diamond fabric paper: K&Company
Iron-on stitch effects: Delta
Love bookplate: 7gypsies
Glue dots: Glue Dots International
Other: Sage, butter cream, and white sheer fabrics; three small white silk roses

Gathered Diagonal

Playing off the peek-a-boo photo of Emily, this scrapbook page drapes a sheer pale gold fabric diagonally across the page. The gold frame gathers the fabric at the center to form two photo mats within a colorblock-style layout. Photos are mounted with foam tape and additional foam tape anchors the fabric to the specialty vellum and white cardstock base. A gold cherub (trimmed from the specialty paper behind the lower right photo) and two crumpled white envelopes that have been brushed with pale inks balance out the arrangement.

Emily at 9 Months

Design: Jill Miller
Photography: Anita Shell Photography
INTERMEDIATE

Specialty vellum: Autumn Leaves
Gold frame: JewelCraft
Parchment pigment inks: ColorBox
Other: White cardstock, pale gold sheer
   fabric, lemon yellow sheer ribbon, two
   small white envelopes, postage stamp

Combining Sheers with Velvet

A single large photo sets the stage for all the design elements to surround it with understated elegance. The Virus family portrait is mounted on black velvet over a white cardstock base. White sheer fabric is draped down the left side of the page and a torn strip of silver-printed vellum is layered on the left. These large design elements are accented with classically styled metal and mirror pieces that add just the right amount of drama to the composition without overwhelming it. The family names are printed on a strip of white cardstock whose seams are hidden under the black and white fabrics.

The Virus Family
Shawne, Randy, Nick, Jessica, Morgan, Piper

The Virus Family

Design: Jill Miller
Photography: Shawne Osterman
BEGINNER

Black velveteen: K&Company
Silver specialty vellum: ColorBox
Love bookplate, chain, black
   leather cording: 7gypsies
Mirror square, silver charm:
   JewelCraft
Other: White cardstock, white
   sheer fabric

Wrapping a Photo Mat

Pale pastel photos can become washed out when scrapped with light colors. Instead, surround your old-fashioned Victorian photos with soft shades of pinks, rose red, and pale olive tones as shown in "Best Friends." For this elegant page, a precut photo mat has been wrapped completely with sheer pink fabric and accented with various jewels, flowers, and threads. A simple knot with a matching printed tag finishes the no-fuss frame; note that the raw edges of the sheer are left exposed. The added dimension makes room for thick page pebbles and fabric roses or any other embellishment you may desire.

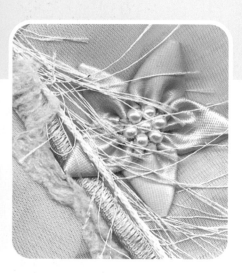

Best Friends

Design: Jill Miller
Photography: Shawne Osterman

BEGINNER

Precut photo mat: Michaels
Specialty paper, tags, jewelry collage kit: Hot Off The Press
Other: Pink cardstock, pink sheer fabric

dare to DREAM

Wrapping the Page

We all know the importance of putting ourselves into our scrapbooks, but sometimes we just find ourselves making excuses not to do it. I just can't get excited about making an "all about me" page, so I created this simple page using a pretty printed sheer fabric wrapped around a white cardstock base with an enlarged photo of me placed in the upper left. I adhered the original photo to a precut photo mat that I had colorized with metallic rub-on creams. Intricate ribbons crisscross over the frame; both the ribbon ends and the raw fabric edges are secured on the back with strapping tape. A quick burnishing to add the rub-on title completes my page and ends my me-page anxiety.

Love to Dream

Design: Jill Miller
Photography: David Thornell
BEGINNER

Printed sheer, embroidered ribbon: Jo-Ann Fabrics
Metallic rub-on creams: Craf-T Products
Rub-on title: Making Memories
Other: White cardstock, printed sheer fabric, precut white photo mat, strapping tape

Babe in Arms

Design: Cary Oliver
Photography: Shaun Austin Photography
BEGINNER

Silver paper: Canson
Nailheads: 7gypsies
Expression sticker: Wordsworth
Other: Brown cardstock, tan sheer fabric, brown embroidery floss

Floss Border

Once again, a simple swath of fabric adds a powerful sense of movement to any scrapbook page. The fabric also provides a good color contrast to Cary's sweet infant photos. Embroidery floss is wrapped around the page and tied in bows to frame the photos. Folded and torn journaling strips fill the open spaces inside the floss frame.back up, placing ribbon just below first stretch of ribbon. Wrap ribbon around back and to the front just below mid-left; wrap around lower right corner, and back to mid-left, just above other stretch of ribbon. Fold ribbon over on the left, secure fold with a nailhead, tuck into left slit, and tape end on back. Add the last nailhead on the bottom to finish the pocket.

Braiden James Stock Feb. 2003

For Thou didst form my inward parts

Thou didst weave me in my mother's womb

I will give thanks to Thee for I am fearfully & wonderfully made.

Side by Side

Design: Jill Miller
Photography: Robert Wagner

ADVANCED

Specialty paper and diecut seals: NRN Designs
"Side by Side" laser-cut title: Deluxe Designs
Other: Gray cardstock, two large ivory tags, wide sheer ribbon with gold wire edges, standard brad, foam tape

Creating a Spinner

There's more than meets the eye here since the center section spins to reveal more photos and the entire "Side by Side" title. To create the spinner, place two tags with holes overlapping and fold each tag in half so the bottom of the tags meet in the center. Fold each half again, reversing the fold so the tag is folded back over itself, cut a 4¼-inch cardstock square, punch a hole in the center, and align over the tag holes. Secure all with a brad and cover the brad with a diecut seal (raise the seal with layers of foam tape). Trim the edges of the sheer ribbon and cut into four squares. Adhere the squares over the spinner (for additional sparkle, as shown in detail) and add photos and title. To finish, adhere ribbon over specialty paper (position two more diecut seals under ribbon, if desired) and adhere remaining diecut seals and photos on both sides of the folded tags as shown.

Sheer Accents

Ian Tribute

Design and photography: Jill Miller

INTERMEDIATE

Printed specialty paper: www.hp.com/go/scrapbooking
Transparency printed attributes: Magic Scraps
Acrylic seals, lettering stickers: Sonnets by Creative
 Imaginations
Thick diamond diecuts: www.thecardladies.com
Metallic rub-on creams: Craf-T Products
Other: Creamy white cardstock; lilac, gold, and lime green
 sheer ribbon; fine sandpaper; foam tape

Highlighting Diagonals

Harlequin-printed paper is accented with three slanted columns of pastel-tinted sheer ribbons that visually anchor the photos and printed

attributes. The translucence of the ribbons leaves the design uninterrupted yet still subdivided into sections, which helps guide the composition. To achieve the white divisions between the diamonds, print the design from the HP scrapbooking website onto cardstock, fold along each diagonal line, and lightly sand the fold until a creamy white edge is exposed. Color the diecut diamonds with rub-on creams for added luminosity.

Harrietta Simms

Design: Cary Oliver
Photographer unknown

BEGINNER

Specialty paper, 3-D
 stickers: K&Company
Other: Kelly green card-
 stock, white vellum,
 3-inch-wide gold sheer
 ribbon, sandpaper
 (optional, for distress-
 ing photo edges)

Ribbon overlay

Cary's tribute to her spirited grandmother Harrietta Simms is full of praise for the endearing character traits that live on in Cary's memory. These attributes have been printed on white vellum and placed under the sheer gold ribbon to help tone down the whiteness, which would have been too distracting without the ribbon overlay. The ribbon ends are secured with layers of stickers so that no adhesive is allowed to detract from the overall beauty of the page.

CHAPTER TWO

Tulle and Lace

Sometimes you may want a delicate sheer that offers a bit of texture. Tulle may be just what you're looking for. The most widely available tulle color is white, but it does come in a wide variety of colors. Lace is another commonly found accent, also sold in a variety of colors, though once again white and ivory are the most popular. Old-fashioned lace is generally found in ivory or off-white and is usually thicker and more substantial than delicate contemporary laces. This chapter presents many different ways to use tulle, new and vintage laces, and even paper lace to enhance photographs, whether fancy or fun. There's even a pet page here with homespun appeal, thanks to a bit of vintage lace.

Tulle

Tulle "Curtain"

Rachael's ballet photo inspired all the design elements on this page. Her tutu colors match the colors of the background paper and stickers, and tulle enhances the theme. Even the satin ribbon is crisscrossed like the ties on her ballet shoes. The tulle has been slit in a "t" or plus-sign pattern, allowing the edges to be folded back like a curtain opened to reveal the photo. Prestrung pearls on fishing wire follow the lines of the upper and lower folds so that a diamond outline naturally frames Rachael's sweet smiling face.

Life Is a Fairy Tale

Design: Jill Miller
Photography: Beth Olsen

INTERMEDIATE

Specialty paper, diecut frame, 3-D stickers: K&Company
Expression word art: Memories Complete
Metal tag: Making Memories
Wire-strung pearls: Michaels
Rose brad: JewelCraft
Other: White tulle, lavender satin ribbon

Tulle Pockets

Cary's baby book tucks neatly into tulle pockets, which serve to hold the book without obscuring any of the design. To create tulle pockets to hold a small book and accent panel, wrap light green cardstock generously with tulle in two layers and secure the edges on the back. To create the pages of the baby book, fold a 12 x 12-inch square of specialty paper in half each way, cut an oval in the center of each quadrant, and layer the pages together. Complete the mini album by adding a ribbon spine, gold photo corners, and an oversized cover.

Cary's Baby Book

Design: Cary Oliver
Photographer unknown

ADVANCED

Specialty paper, diecut oval frames, green satin bows: Anna Griffin
Charms, gold photo corners: JewelCraft
Expression sticker: Wordsworth
Other: Light and darker green cardstocks, white tulle, green satin ribbon

Doily Border

Old-fashioned doilies are typically used as placemats for dining room tables or accents placed beneath vases or knickknacks, yet they make perfect photo mats and borders for classic Victorian portraits and scrapbook pages. Enhance their soft appeal by placing them on top of crushed dark velveteen and next to satin ribbons and antique gold accents. Pearl trim and a vintage-look charm completes the nineteenth-century look.

Great Grandma Busby

Design: Cary Oliver
Photographer unknown
BEGINNER

Burgundy ribbon and velveteen: K&Company
Antique gold frame, charm: JewelCraft
Other: Old-fashioned lace doily, pearl trim, olive green wide satin ribbon

Lace

Lace "Railing"

A century ago in home decor, rooms often had painted wooden picture railings running the length of the room about 12 inches below the ceiling. These railings supported all of the paintings and photographs that were hung with rope or wire from pegs imbedded into the wood. Playing off this heritage style, Cary has hung her photos from buttons mounted on a paper picture railing that has been trimmed with lace and accented with gold threads and lace. A pull-down advertisement of this little Italian dress shop hides the journaling. In this context, even the specialty paper takes on the look of antique wallpaper, augmenting the overall vintage style of the pqge.

Burano Lace

Design and photography: Cary Oliver
ADVANCED

Specialty paper: Family Archives
Gold lettering stickers: Frances Meyer
Other: Gold and burgundy papers, wide white lace trim, gold ribbon, gold roping, old-fashioned buttons, thread

Lace and Tag Accents

The wonderfully warm ivory color of old-fashioned lace can add subtle interest to a page that could easily be overpowered by a bright white lace. "Piciotto" plays the mottled tan of the tags against various kids of ivory lace. The layers of the page gradually darken to draw the viewer into the composition. This page also shows a good way to fill in the open space of a photograph with a design element when cropping the photo would be undesirable. Look for opportunities to keep your photos full size whenever possible and you'll find yourself pulled into the design details.

Piciotto

Design and photography:
Jill Miller

BEGINNER

Leatherette papers:
 K&Company
Large walnut and small collage
 tags: Rusty Pickle
Vellum expression: Memories
 Complete
Other: Old-fashioned lace,
 wooden heart, red paint

Paper Doily Backdrop

This elegant yet easy scrapbook page can be made in minutes thanks to the large paper-lace doily turned on point, and the small silk flowers. Even the floral spray takes just a second to bend into the corners of the page. To add more photos and journaling, mount your matted photo onto a folded piece of $8^{1}/_{2}$ x $5^{1}/_{2}$-inch cardstock to create a photo book. Be sure to use a spray adhesive to attache your doily to minimize any torn edges.

Our Wedding Day

Design: Jill Miller
Photography: David Labrum
BEGINNER

Silk flowers: Michaels
Floral stickers: PrintWorks
Other: Light blue and darker blue
cardstocks (for base), aqua and
white cardstocks (for photo book),
8-inch-square paper-lace doily,
spray adhesive, glue dots

Paper-Lace Envelopes

Design: Carolyn Holt and Jill Miller
BEGINNER

Sunflower stickers;
blue sponge paper;
heart stamp; black,
red, and gold ink;
expression stamp:
PrintWorks
Other: Yellow, white,
and pink card-
stocks; 8-inch
square paper-lace
doilies; gold-wired
sheer ribbon, spray
adhesive

Doily Envelope and Gift Box

Need a quick card and envelope or a small gift box? These samples are perfect. To construct, turn the doily on point and fold each triangular portion into the center of the doily so they slightly overlap one another. To make the doily work as a tiny gift box, first mount the doily with spray adhesive onto cardstock and then fold as before. Wrap the box with ribbon to keep it closed and finish with a simple stamped heart or a sticker. A decorated panel with a stamped expression easily slides in and out when you leave one section of the doily unsecured.

Paper Lace

Layered doily surround

The construction of this scrapbook page is just a few steps beyond "Our Wedding Day," shown opposite. Notice that the corrugated paper is the element now turned on point while the doily is centered within the preprinted frame of the specialty paper. Twig and ivy stickers form the photo frame and the opening has been cut along the sticker profile. Another 8-inch doily is cut into quarters (at center midpoint of all sides), spread apart, and positioned *under* the edges of the corrugated paper. The doily on top of the corrugated paper will cover the sections of the cut doily. Remember to add your photo behind the opening before securing all the elements to the page.

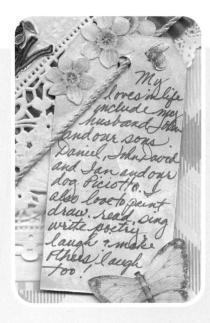

CHAPTER THREE

Snaps, Beads, Bags, and Charms

Beads, charms, and other little add-ons can lend quite a bit of sparkle to your scrapbook pages in no time at all. Snaps are easy to fit into small holes poked through your paper, and micro beads are simply shaken over designs whose surfaces have been covered with crystal lacquer. Once dry, the lacquer bonds the beads in place. Adding a lovely beaded ribbon straight from the fabric store requires no more than laying down a strip of double-stick tape. And using fabric bags of all kinds—muslin bags, sheer fabric bags, even large bags made from handmade mulberry papers—injects scrapbook pages with all kinds of possibilities. Scrapbooking "jewelry" finds its spotlight in this chapter, but look throughout the book for many other designs incorporating these wonderful embellishments.

Snaps and Beads

Renaissance Faire

Design and photography: Jill Miller

INTERMEDIATE

Two-sided green/light green cardstock: Paper
    Adventures
Flourish stamp, mini brads: Making Memories
Gold Brilliance ink: Tsukineko
Gold photo corners, gold paper: Canson
Red-and-gold puffy hearts: Marcel Schurman
Wonder Tape: Ranger Industries
36-inch beaded ribbon: JewelCraft
Other: Clear crystals, craft knife, straightedge

Double-Sided Page

This double-spread scrapbook page makes the most of two-sided cardstock by cutting a window. To create this window, use a craft knife and straightedge to cut 5 x 5-inch slits in the shape of a letter X. Fold back each triangle thus created, then fold forward the tips of each one. Adhere a small crystal to the folded tips, add gold paper, mount the photos, and accent with gold photo corners. On the darker green side of the cardstock, cut the gold paper in half, add puffy hearts, and affix a journaling panel under the flaps. With Wonder Tape and mini brads, mount a 13-inch strip of beaded ribbon for an accent on each page as shown. Strip beads from remaining ribbon and adhere with Wonder Tape to pages as shown.

Micro Beads

Pretty pink princesses are surrounded by jeweled accents and metallic shimmer that took less time to add than the girls took to primp and pose for their photos! Start by painting the top title with a pink paint pen and the shadow title with silver. The paint dries instantly so you can adhere the two titles together and mount on the page right away. Layer all the elements on the page and coat all the exposed edges of the photos and accents with lacquer as shown. Sprinkle all lacquered areas with the micro beads and let dry.

Celebrate

Design: Jill Miller
Photography: Melodie Jones
ADVANCED

Pink/green plaid, purple, and pink cardstocks: PrintWorks
Pink and silver metallic paint pens: Marvy
Celebrate title, butterflies, heart border: Lil Davis Designs
Clear crystal lacquer: Sakura
Pink metallic "Beadazzles": Suze Weinburg

Designing with Snaps

Three small photos from a contact sheet fill the lower precut squares of the cardstock, enhanced with superfine silver thread that creates a diamond frame over each photo. Poke the cardstock with evenly spaced holes, fasten a snap into each one, and string fine thread from snap to snap, nestling the thread between the two sections of each snap. Create the mat behind each photo with a wide strip of smoothed-out raffia that is wrapped on each side of all the openings. Accordion-fold the remaining raffia and sew the spine to make the mini book. More snaps and silver thread unite the book with the overall design of the page.

My True Love, My Emily

Design: Jill Miller
Photography: Mars Meyer
ADVANCED

Precut window cardstock, metal letters: Making Memories
Fabric lattice paper: K&Company
Other: Small sewing snaps, fine silver thread, wide pink raffia

Hong Kong Harbor

Design: Jill Miller
Photography: David Thornell
BEGINNER
Red script -style
  specialty paper:
  Club Scrap
Iron-on transfer paper:
  Hewlett-Packard
Other: 5x7-inch muslin
  bag, sandpaper, iron

Photo Transfer

This muslin bag is perfect for storing all those travel tickets, admission stubs, and other relevant ephemera. To add the photo, simply print your photo on iron-on transfer paper, trim it to size, sand the edges, and iron it face down on muslin following the manufacturer's directions on the transfer paper package. Allow the image to cool before slowly and carefully peeling off the paper backing, checking for thorough photo adherence. If any part of the image did not adhere properly, reapply heat (with paper backing back in place) and allow to cool again.

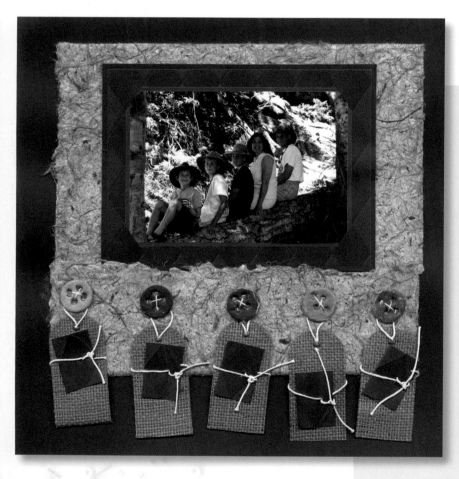

Hidden Pouch

At first it may be hard to spot the fabric pouch, but look closely and you'll see the torn edge of the flap just below the photo mat. This rustic textural pouch is a perfect complement for this outdoor photo as well as for the trail maps and additional photos stored inside. To make the tiny trifolds that are tied with twine on the burlap tags, diecut five tags from specialty paper and five from burlap. Journal on the reverse of each paper tag as desired. Fold the paper tags into thirds, wrap with twine, thread twine through burlap tag holes, and tie loose knots to close paper tags as shown.

Log Family

Design: Jill Miller
Photography: David Thornell
INTERMEDIATE
Handmade paper pouch with
  buttons: Stampington
Harlequin-printed specialty
  paper: K&Company
Tag diecutting tool:
  Sizzix:Ellison
Other: Burgundy cardstock,
  burlap, twine

Fabric Bags

Double Pockets

This monochromatic layout takes its color cue from the sweet photos of little Emily Rose. The composition is split down the center: on the right a sheer pink fabric bag mounted on a torn and folded vellum pocket holds Emily's photo; the left side features a reduced photocopy of a song titled "Emily." To allow viewers to see the other side of the sheet music, it has been tucked inside a long vellum pocket created by securing bottom and sides of the vellum to the page. If desired, add ribbon stitching to circle tag and attach it to the top of the music sheet for easy removal from pocket.

Emily Rose Song

Design: Jill Miller
Photography: Mars Meyer

ADVANCED

Specialty paper, pink vellum: Family Archives
Premade stitched ribbon: Magic Scraps
Rub-on letters, circle tags: Making Memories
Alphabet dies, mini hole punch: Sizzix:Ellison
4x5-inch pink sheer fabric: Pouches Bag-It
Other: Sheet music, thin rose pink ribbon

Muslin Bag

"Cousins" is a wonderful example of how to add collage details and journaling to a page without overpowering the photos. Here a small muslin bag holds a trifold book made from a money envelope to contain all the delicious details of the events surrounding this photo. Simple attribute stickers, printed twill tape, and gold charms dress up the plain bag and anchor the photo to the page. Everywhere touches of gold add a bit of shimmer to all things shabby chic—even the cardstock base, handmade paper, and photo edges have been brushed with gold.

Cousins

Design: Jill Miller
Photography: Anita Shell

ADVANCED

Handmade paper: Creative Imaginations
Money envelope, charms: American Tag Company
Printed twill tape: Me & My Big Ideas
All stickers: K&Company
Gold and Orchid Opalite inks: Tsukineko
Other: Tan cardstock, muslin bag, gold organza ribbon

Charms

A babe in the house
is a well-spring
of pleasure,
a messenger
of peace & love,
a resting place
for innocence
on earth;
a link between
angels and
men.
— *Tupper*

bliss

peace

love

adore

spirit

dream

wish

believe

3 months

9 months

divine

family

I'm finally here!
Charlotte Bryn South
October 25, 2002
Proud parents: Brett and Sarah South

She's Finally Here!

Design: Jill Miller
Birth announcement
design: Brett South
BEGINNER

Attribute printed rimmed
   nailheads:
   www.foofala.com
Pink specialty paper: Rusty
   Pickle
Expression sticker:
   Wordsworth
Other: Translucent light-
   weight white felt

Nailhead Accents

After waiting nine months for Charlotte to arrive, I didn't want
to wait nine minutes longer to scrap and send this special
announcement scrapbook page to my sister Sarah. The cleverly
cut windows in the translucent material help to frame their
clever baby announcement. The window on the left is made by
cutting 3-inch slits in the shape of an X; the middle one is the
same size but formed as a upside down T. The windows on the
right resemble a 4-inch capital I with top and bottom rows of
differing lengths. All the flaps are folded back and secured in
place with decorative nailheads. See the next chapter for even
more ways to get fuzzy effects with felt.

adore

Shimmering Accents

Once again, sparkle and shine are seen not just in Charlotte's pretty face but in the gold charms, shimmering ribbons, gold-inked frames, and a background paper that has been brushed with gold, white, and blue opalescence inks. Shimmery ribbon visually links the little frames, creating a subtle vertical down the page. The embossed shells create subtle detail on the page but can be omitted if time is tight. To speed along the construction of the page I trimmed all four photos to 3½ inches square, but let your photos dictate the size and cropping for your own design.

Beach Baby Charlotte

Design and photography: Jill Miller
INTERMEDIATE

Gold charms, 1-inch ribbon, mini brad: JewelCraft
Swirl frames: Chatterbox
Teal ribbed cardstock, vellum: Paper Adventures
Shimmer white, blue, and gold Opalite inks: Tsukineko
Lettering and expression stickers: Creative Imaginations
Embosser, shell embossing template: Lasting Impressions

Softening Photo Edges

Ian is truly a blessing to our family and so this page honors his spunk and spirit rather than the beach theme seen in the landscape of the photo. Give yourself the liberty to journal those feelings that your photos evoke rather than focus solely on the various events surrounding your subjects. Also note the misty edges of the photos, which is easy to create. Just dab the edges of the glossy photo prints with a baby wipe and then place one-ply facial tissue into the damp areas. Even when dry, the tissue will stay in place.

Blessing

Design and photography: Jill Miller
ADVANCED

Sonnets specialty papers: Creative Imaginations
Glossy photo paper: Hewlett-Packard
Faux wax seal, gold charm: Creative Imaginations
Laser-cut title: www.sarahheidt-photocrafts.com
Other: Baby wipe, facial tissues, ribbons

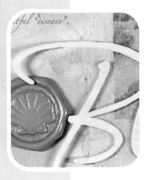

CHAPTER FOUR

Woven Fabrics, Fur, and Felt

This chapter is all about texture. Every fabric showcased here is loaded with texture, from burlap to beach mats, fabric mesh to metal mesh, faux fur to fuzzy felt. A wide variety of everyday events and a few staged settings will lend as much style to all those average-day photos as to your portrait shots. First we'll use woven fabrics such as colored gauze, burlap, and reed. Next we'll explore the more open weaves found in Magic Mesh (a plastic self-adhesive material), metal mesh, and even beach mats! Finally we'll check out faux fur and felt, which is just plain fun to add to your scrapbook pages. Since all these materials vary in thickness and texture, keep in mind that you may have to frame your page in a shadowbox or heavy-duty sheet protector. Be sure to keep plenty of glue dots handy when working with all of these materials.

Gathered Corner Bands

Rather than crop this off-center photograph of her great-grandfather, Cary chose to add roughly gathered gauze fabric and 3-D stickers over the opposing corners, which reinforces the diagonal composition. To easily create the many gathers, run your fabric strips though the adhesive machine. While you're at it, you can also run your punch letters through the machine to use up the empty space on each side of your fabric strip. Adhere these letters over the tin squares and stitch them together with green floss as shown. If you don't have an adhesive machine you can create the gathers with a basting stitch, or lay down double-stick tape and scrunch up the fabric along the tape line.

Rugged

Design: Cary Oliver
Photographer unknown
BEGINNER

Checked fabric paper, 3-D stickers, leather paper: K&Company
Metal stitching squares: Making Memories
EAtoZy punch letters: Scrapsakes
Adhesive machine: Xyron
Other: Green heavy-weight gauze, green embroidery floss

Woven Fabrics

Burlap Mat

County casual is the style of scrapbook page, reflecting the trendy colors of the late 1970s, when this photo was taken. Dark brown, sunny yellow, and bright orange provide quite a bit of contrast and character. With every third string removed, Cary's clever burlap mat makes use of the extra burlap scraps, and along with raffia and simple silk flowers, she has created a beautiful page for barely a buck or two.

Harvest Festival

Design: Cary Oliver
Photographer unknown
BEGINNER

Other: Yellow cardstock; brown burlap; orange, yellow, and plain raffia; silk flowers

Rustic Accents

Precut grid paper helps fill this page easily with photos, placed above and below one big title that spans the page. Lettering stickers are the easiest way to add a title to the bumpy burlap, but be sure to add a mini glue dot to each letter to keep it from falling off the page (that's what happened to the "s" in Cary's title)! The border around the page is made from torn strips of faux-leather paper and the triangles of real leather scraps add yet another touch of texture to this rough-and-ready cowboy-themed creation.

Little Boy, Big Boots

Design and photography: Cary Oliver
BEGINNER

Colorblocking grid paper: Die Cuts with a View
Faux-leather paper: Provo Craft
Lettering stickers: Cut-It-Up
Other: Burlap and leather scraps, glue dots

Textural Effects

Have you ever shot a full roll of film during one fantastic afternoon and find that you wanted to scrap every one of the twenty-four pictures? Cary's photo-filled page shows you how. Close-up details and faraway shots are all included. Note too that one photo spans two squares; can you find it? Cary also has added ivory gauze and letter-embossed vellum strips in order to keep the focus on the photos and yet include lots of journaling and texture.

Newport Beach

Design and photography: Cary Oliver
INTERMEDIATE

Reed covered frame: Westrim
Ecru vellum: PrintWorks
Lettering labeler: Dymo
Square punch: Marvy
Other: Light brown cardstock, ivory lightweight gauze, small seashells

Mats and Mesh

Noah and Grammie

Design and photography:
Cary Oliver

INTERMEDIATE

Seahorse laser-cuts: Lil Davis
Lettering stickers: Creative
 Imaginations
Expression sticker:
 Wordsworth
Decorating Chalks: Craf-T
 Products
Other: White cardstock,
 woven beach mat or place-
 mat, artificial seaweed

Beach Mat Background

I had a very hard time trying to decide whether this page should go into the next chapter, "Salvage Scrapbooking," because the background is entirely made up of a woven beach mat. You can also use a placemat if you don't have a beach mat on hand (or yours is just too sandy). Trim the mat to the desired size and mount on cardstock. Use the leftover twig scraps to frame your photos. Adhere the expression sticker over a landscape photo; add chalk to your seahorses; and adhere the title, photos, and seaweed accents with glue dots. Artificial seaweed is available in craft stores or wherever aquarium supplies are sold.

Plastic Mesh Detail

Notice the linear composition of the page and how the large photo on the right is balanced by the layered textural elements on the left. Uniting the two sides is a freehand title cut from olive cardstock that spans the darker tones of the page. Although plastic mesh cannot be manipulated like metal mesh, it is nevertheless soft and pliable. Here it adds a masculine edginess that compliments this young man's dressed-up demeanor. Look closely at his feet and you'll see that Johnny still likes to go casual and just be himself.

Johnny

Design: Jill Miller
Photography: Beth Olsen
INTERMEDIATE
Gold Magic Mesh, nailheads: JewelCraft
Script fabric, leather papers: K&Company
Other: Dark brown and olive green cardstocks, craft knife

Sisters Sweet

Design: Jill Miller
Photography: Shawne Osterman
ADVANCED
Metal mesh: Scrapyard 329
Pink striped and solid papers: PrintWorks
Expression sticker: Wordsworth
Buttons, leaves, knit floral accents: Hot Off The Press
Other: White cardstock, sheer green tone-on-tone fabric

Metal Mesh Adornments

"Sisters Sweet" is sewn directly onto a cardstock base, but you can also construct this page with tape, fusible webbing, or glue. Once you've covered the cardstock base with fabric, cut out a large square in the center, glue the frayed edges of the opening to the cardstock, and cover up the edges with four strips of wire mesh. Curl individual wires taken from the mesh to string buttons and accents onto the mesh frame anywhere you desire.

Fringed Framing

Though it may not be evident in the illustration, this page is very thick and therefore resides in a shadowbox frame hung in Johnny's bedroom. To create the photo frame, draw a 4 x 6-inch frame in the center of an 8-inch leather square and sew or glue the leather to the cow print along the inner frame outline. Next, cut slits all along each side of the leather to create the fringed edge and remove overlapping slitted sections at each corner. Adhere a photo in the center and secure the cow print to a cardstock base. Cut a bandana in half along the diagonal and roll each section from the top to the point of the triangle. Tie the ends together and glue the bandana halves over the leather frame as shown.

Cowboy Johnny

Design and photography: Beth Olsen

ADVANCED

Other: Brown cardstock, cow-print faux fur, tan leather, bandana, glue dots or sewing machine, very sharp scissors

Faux Fur and Felt

Felt Embellishment

To create your own part-digital, part-paper-scrapped page, first import your photos into your photo editing software program. Enlarge, reduce, and add edge effects as desired. Type the title in two sections and add an embossed text filter to the last line of the title. Add journaling as desired and print on 12 x 12-inch matte finish photo paper using a wide-format printer. Sew strips of felt into 4 x 2-inch cuffs; add red buttons and acrylic lettering pebbles if desired. Stitch a large piece of red felt to a white cardstock base. Glue all elements to the print as shown, then mount the print to the base.

Little Lady in Red

Design: Jill Miller

Photography: Epson

INTERMEDIATE

Photoshop Elements software: Adobe
12 x 12-inch matte-finish photo paper, 1280 wide-format printer: Epson
Lettering page pebbles: Making Memories
Other: White cardstock, red felt, red buttons, sewing machine

Our Little Lady in Red

l a u r e n *loves her red hat and coat. If there is just a nip of frost in the air, Lauren has her hat and coat all buttoned up. Her pretty red lips and blushing cheeks perfectly match her favorite winter coverup and we can't help but smile right along with her. New Years Day 2002*

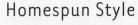

Homespun Style

A country Christmas greeting needs only a few felt mittens, a bit of raffia, a small tied tag, and some earth-toned plaids to perfectly preserve this memory. Blue cardstock serves as a photo mat; yellow cardstock forms the tag. Intricate cutting of embossed recesses in the cardstock opens up wonderful windows for a clever sticker title and makes a nice frame for one adorable stitched mitten. Another row of slits following the lines of the pre-embossed cardstock makes it easy to thread rows of raffia to add to the homespun style of this scrapbook page.

Home Sweet Home

Design: Jill Miller
Photography: Jeff Jensen
INTERMEDIATE

Green embossed cardstock, plaid embossed vellum, lettering stickers: K&Company

Stitched felt mittens, rope, clothespins: Westrim Crafts

Raffia: Marvy

Other: Blue and yellow cardstock, craft knife, ruler, cutting mat

CHAPTER FIVE

Salvage Scrapbooking

This chapter is one of my favorites, since as a dedicated yard sale enthusiast, I am always finding "dirt cheap" materials for some cute, clever, and sometimes quirky scrapbook pages. You will see pages created from materials found in closets, on cupboard shelves, and even across the bathroom counter! Shirts, jeans, overalls, and onesies; shower curtains, towels, and tissues are all incorporated on these pages. Despite the salvage character, each of these pages has sentimental value, and the tongue-in-cheek approach adds even more fun as you strive to preserve your meaningful memories.

Onesies and Jumpers

Mesh Bag Treasure Keeper

A poem written just for Emily, a small photo of her, and a pressed flower are adhered to a mica tile tag with decoupage medium. A mesh bag preserves her birthday jumper. Even a large white button has a portion of a pressed flower decoupaged and placed on the tag. The title is printed on a nonembossed piece of button-themed background paper and secured to just the underside of the flap on the fabric bag. Additional buttons help to coordinate the bag with the overall design of the page.

Emily Button Bag

Design: Jill Miller
Photography: Kim Meyer
ADVANCED
Embossed and nonembossed button background papers: K&Company
Mica tiles, decoupage medium: US Art Quest
Mesh bag: Stampington
Other: Infant jumper, pressed flowers, buttons

Featuring Keepsakes

Emily's parents treasure this sentimental page because on it are stored Emily's first-day photos, baby booties, cap, and cotton onesie. Simple layers and crochet flowers that divide the photos add interest yet do not overpower the important keepsakes that can be seen both in the photos and on the page itself. Consider preserving your keepsakes along with your photos so that you can keep all your priceless mementos in one place.

Emily Dream

Design: Jill Miller
Photography: Mars Meyer
BEGINNER

Glossy pink cardstock: NRN Designs
Crochet flowers: EK Success
Wire word, heart tag: Creative Imaginations
Other: Infant onesie, booties, knit cap

Self-Contained Pockets

This keepsake page is similar to "Emily Dream" in its design concept, yet if you look closely you'll see two clever pockets. The first, along the button row, is made by simply folding up the midsection of a jumper until it fits on the cardstock base and adhering buttons with glue dots to cover the fold. Before adhering the finished outfit to the page, remember to cut out four tags in descending sizes from the cardstock and then cover the holes with your outfit. Three tags are readily apparent but again, look closely. The fourth tag is hidden in the neck opening of the jumper. This is the second pocket, which allows you to tuck away more personal journaling or "revealing" photos.

Emily Jumper

Design: Jill Miller
Photography: Mars Meyer
INTERMEDIATE

Stitched background paper: Westrim
Button and wire collage kit: Westrim
Nested tag stencil: Hot Off The Press
Other: Infant jumper

Preserving an Outfit

"Baby Blues" not only features an adorable photo but also preserves a little girl's favorite outfit for her to enjoy for years to come. Cut off the top portion and the straps of the overalls; secure them on the back of the cardstock, and position rose stickers as desired. The only time-consuming part involves making the title block. Bubble font letters are printed on white cardstock and "blues" is handwritten and cut out from the thick areas of the title lettering. A quick swipe or two of blue ink matches the title to the denim.

Baby Blues

Design: Jill Miller
Photography: Beth Olsen
BEGINNER

3-D glitter stickers: K&Company
Tag, spiral clip: American Tag Company
Royal blue ink: ColorBox
Other: Toddler-size blue jean overalls, white cardstock, craft knife, cutting mat

Denim

Cary

Design: Cary Oliver
Photographer unknown
BEGINNER

Denim diecut and frame:
  My Minds Eye
Diecut letters: Sizzix: Ellison
Other: Paper bandana ribbon, rope, straw mat

Faux Denim

A quick fabric fix can be seen in Cary's childhood scrapbook page. A close look reveals that the photo frame and diecut heart are really faux-denim paper accents. The bandana accent is also just stiffened paper ribbon. The rope and straw, on the other hand, are real, but strewn freely about the layout.

Recycled Jeans

To stretch your scrapbooking dollar, try scrapping a page using just bits and pieces of fabrics and twine that you already have on hand. Create photo mats and a tag from cardstock, add a few simple stickers and one cool dog tag, and you'll have a scrapbook spread for next to nothing. If you cut up an old denim shirt, be sure to include the shirt pocket and fold over the shirttails for additional interest. Hinge a few plaid squares to create photo flaps and additional journaling space if desired. Nailheads easily secure multiple layers of fabric to your heavy cardstock base.

Dog Days

Design and photography:
Cary Oliver

INTERMEDIATE

Lettering stickers, paws:
   Cut It Up
Metal dog tag, nailheads:
   American Tag Company
Other: Thick cardstock,
   navy and white card-
   stocks, blue denim and
   plaid fabric scraps,
   twine, tiny clothespins

Getting Down to Business

What better way to scrapbook all those business cards and workplace photos gathered through the years than literally on a work shirt and tie? Cary's page is sure to be remembered by both her family and her scrapbooking friends. The journaling for this clever creation is tucked into the dressmaker's label on the underside of the tie and the business cards can be pulled right out of the pocket protector. It's so easy to create your own wonderful workplace page. Just tuck a stiff cardstock into the shirt, trim off the back of the shirt (to reduce bulk), and tape the raw edges to the back of the page. Perhaps the hardest part will be tying the tie!

Work Shirt

Design: Cary Oliver
Photographer unknown

INTERMEDIATE

Men's dress shirt, tie, handkerchief: Nordstrom
Other: White cardstock

Closet Creations

Travelogue

Did you know that you can turn just about any shirt into a scrapbook pocket page? Check out how Cary's simple cotton blouse has been fitted over a stiff cardstock base and folded up on itself at the bottom to create a pocket to hold lots of travel memorabilia and a mini flip photo book, which has been accented with modeling paste and pearlized paint. The embroidered leather belt found during her travels adds a decorative banner to the top of her playful pocket. Next time you are canvassing the local yard sales, look for light-weight shirts like this. You don't even have to worry if they are too sheer for actual wearing—they still make a great scrapbook accent.

Swiss Miss Blouse

Design and photography: Cary Oliver
INTERMEDIATE

Cardstock, specialty paper: K&Company
Travels diecut: The Paper Loft
Modeling paste: US Art Quest
Pearl Ex pigments: Jacquard Products
Other: Cotton blouse, embroidered belt, map, flip photo album, travel brochures

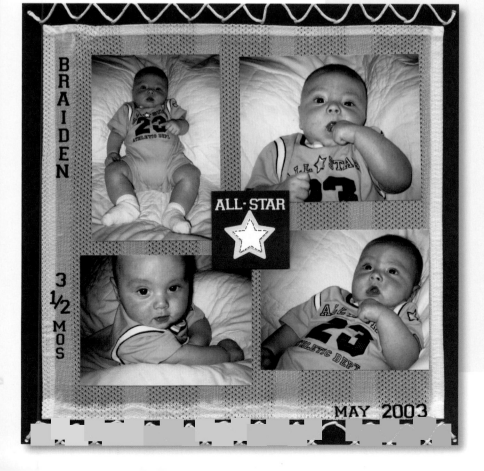

Mesh Shirt Ground

This simple scrapbook page uses a mesh-striped athletic shirt for its fabric background. Just trim your shirt to your desired size, allowing an extra 1/4 inch on all sides. Turn back the 1/4 extra along each side and either sew your shirt directly to your background cardstock or adhere the edges with tape. To echo the yellow of Braiden's jumper, Cary has threaded bright yellow cording through holes she punched along the top and bottom of the page. Take a look through your own closet to see what might work on a scrapbook page!

Braiden All-Star

Design: Cary Oliver
Photography: Shaun Austin Photography
BEGINNER

Alphabet stickers: Paper Craft
1/8-inch hole punch, star punch: Marvy
Yellow cording: JewelCraft
Other: Athletic shirt, sewing machine or double-stick tape

Shower Curtain Scraps

Inspiration can strike anywhere, even while taking a shower! Many creative types daydream during a hot shower but this page shows what happens when you open your eyes and look up. The criss-crossed white panels are stripped from the top of a heavy cotton shower curtain. The metal grommets make perfect frames for small photos and the glossy fish (made with UTEE and pigment ink) and rhinestones complement the reflections in the surf. Be sure to take advantage of open spaces in your photos by adding rub-on words directly in those spaces.

Surfer Boy

Design and photography: Jill Miller
INTERMEDIATE

Fish foam stamp: Rubber Stampede
Teal and blue ink: Ranger
Ultra-thick embossing powder (UTEE): Suze Weinberg
White rub-on words: Making Memories
Other: Light blue cardstock, top banner of grommeted shower curtain, rhinestones

Character

Design and photography: Jill Miller
ADVANCED

Laser-cut title:
    www.sarahheidtphotocrafts.com
Glimmer chalks: Craf-T Products
Metal mesh: Scrapyard 329
Metal letters: Making Memories
Expression sticker: Wordsworth
Glue sticks: Avery
Other: Powder blue cardstock, facial tissues

Texturing with Tissues

Sitting on your bathroom counter is yet another scrapbooking supply. Facial tissues can add texture to your work. All you need is your trusty glue stick and a colored cardstock base. Separate the tissues into single plies and tear into strips. Apply glue stick randomly all over the cardstock and place torn tissue strips on the glue. Layer as desired and let dry. Add a laser-cut title, wire mesh (adhere under the photo and at the top with metal letters and mini brads), and expression sticker as shown. To deepen contrasts and add shimmering color, accent with glimmer chalks as shown in this cool, edgy scrapbook page.

Bathroom Beauties

Terrycloth Mats

Emily's pale pink cheeks and her purple terrycloth towel provide the inspiration for the purple vellum background and white terrycloth photo mats. Fuzzy white yarn lends horizontal strength at the bottom of the composition. Shiny silver increase the shimmer begun by the purple accents that have been added to the printed swirl vellum by drawing over the designs with a glue pen and dusting lightly with pigment powders. Even the precut window frames shimmer with purple powders, which have been dusted over double-stick tape.

Pixie

Design: Jill Miller
Photography: Mars Meyer

ADVANCED

Pale plum cardstock: Bazzill
Terrycloth, white yarn: Jo-Ann Fabrics
Precut window-frame cardstock: Making Memories
Purple Pearl Ex shimmering pigment powders: Jacquard Products
Specialty swirl and pastel purple vellum: ColorBox
Metal letters, words, photo corners: Making Memories
Glue pen: Zig
Other: Double-stick tape

Squeaky Clean

Design: Jill Miller
Photography: Sarah South

INTERMEDIATE

Specialty paper, fabric paper, translucent fabric papers, stickers: K&Company
Oval metal tag: Making Memories
Other: Terrycloth towel, Black permanent pen

Toweled Background

Few things are cuter than a sweet little baby all wrapped up just out of the tub. Take a photo and then wrap up a wonderful scrapbook page with the very same terrycloth towel. Colored fabric papers offset the stark white towel (peeking out under the CLEAN letter stickers) and visually complement the photo. For great photo mats that allow the underlying specialty papers to peek through yet don't compete with the photo, select translucent fabric papers that only ghost back the design of your specialty paper. Be sure to check out the next chapter for even more inspiration on working with fabric papers.

CHAPTER SIX

No-Sew Fabric Creations

Everyone loves the touch and feel of fabrics but not everyone loves to sew. Happily, you won't need a needle and thread for any of the pages in this chapter. All of these fabrics have been adhered with tape or glue or their own self-adhesive backing. Leather scraps, pre-embossed sheets, and faux leather also "pony up" to the task. You'll see a range of techniques, from easy to advanced, to enhance your fabric papers, beginning with simpler techniques like matching plain velveteen papers or chalk painting pre-embossed velveteen. Then it's on to slightly more complex methods like iron stamping, iron-on appliqués, and fabric painting. Plaids, dots, and even embossed wallpaper samples round out our potluck collection of fabric ideas.

Leather

Electronic Embellishments

To create the look of leather without the thickness (or the expense), use a baby wipe to rag-roll a spectrum of brown and sepia tones onto tan cardstock. Faux leather is also printable—just be sure to mark off the area where your photo will go before you compose your journaling in the software. Print a draft first; once you're satisfied with the placement, feed your inked masterpiece through the printer. Create a flag from the torn shapes within the software under the Shapes tab and add text to the flag as shown. To make the title, click on Add Text, type "My Country 'Tis of Thee," rotate 90 degrees, and enlarge to print full length of paper. Duplicate title, change color to red, and reduce text box until only half of the red is visible. Layer over blue title, then print, trim, and tear elements and ink all edges as desired. Brush more inks onto all remaining page elements and tear edges to unify the overall antique theme.

My Country 'Tis of Thee

Design: Jill Miller
Photographer unknown

ADVANCED

Scrapbooking software: HP Creative Scrapbook Assistant
Specialty paper, walnut tag: Rusty Pickle
Colorblock blue grid: Diecuts with a View
Cappuccino Kaleidacolor inks: Tsukineko
"My Grandfather" subtitle: Karen Foster
Other: Tan and ivory cardstocks, baby wipes, glue stick

Leather-and-Suede Look

Real leather embossing requires a hammer, embossing plates, and lots of patience. Fortunately, manufacturers now sell pre-embossed leather to make Western-themed pages come alive with authentic-looking detail. For the photo frame, cut ½-inch strips of cardstock, wrap with suede, and secure with Supertape. To disguise the joins in the frame strips, create custom photo corners from scraps of leather and suede secured with nailheads. For the strong vertical, hole-punch along both edges of a rectangle of tan suede, then thread it with a thin leather strip to mimic the stitching on an old-fashioned saddle. Finish off the rustic layout with leather photo corners and adhere all elements to leather background to finish.

Cowboy Up

Design: Cary Oliver
Photographer: unknown
INTERMEDIATE

Tan suede, pre-embossed leather, nailheads, metal letters, circle charm: K&Company
Leather strips (from a purchased belt)
Walnut tag: 7gypsies
½-inch Supertape: Therm O Web
⅛-inch hole punch: Marvy
Other: Cardstock

Cowboy Noah

Design: Jill Miller
Photography: Cary Oliver
INTERMEDIATE

Sizzix tag diecut: Ellison
Metal letters: Creative Imaginations
Silver paint pen: Marvy
Glue dots: Therm O Web
Other: Heavy cardstock, leather scraps, metal conchos, sandpaper

Distressed Leather

This fun page has no wrong way to do it. You need only a small variety of scrap leathers, a few little embellishments, and some sandpaper. Arrange your scraps to cover your cardstock base and mark the places where the leather edges overlap. Remove the leather scraps one at a time, and trim leather along markings with a sharp craft knife. Before cutting all the way through, try ripping a few to get some cool frayed edges. Replace leather and adhere each piece to cardstock base. Diecut your tag from another scrap of leather, cut holes for dimensional metal letters as shown (to help prevent indentations in the facing scrapbook page), and journal with a silver paint pen. Lightly sand photo edges and adhere to page to finish.

For Time

and all Eternity

Pre-embossed Velveteen

The tone-on-tone pale reds provide a strong visual anchor for the diamond-mounted watch charms and yet still allow the large photograph to take center stage. To add the metallic touch, apply antique gold rub-on cream to the diamond diecuts, then seal with spray fixative; affix the self-adhesive watch charms. Cut around the floral profile of the embossed velveteen, arrange it on the page, then secure the diamond diecuts over and under the meandering velvet. Because only a portion of the velveteen is used, try colorizing the extra for another project, as seen below in "A Boy's Will."

For Time and all Eternity

Design: Jill Miller
Photography: David Labrum
BEGINNER

Specialty paper, puffy plastic watch
    charms, pre-embossed velveteen:
    K&Company
Thick diamond diecuts:
    www.thecardladies.com
Gold metallic rub-on creams: Craf-T
    Products
Other: Spray fixative

A Boy's Will

Design and photography: Jill Miller
INTERMEDIATE

Pre-embossed velveteen: K&Company
Decorating chalks, E-Z Enhancer, Pixie
    and Pudgy applicators: Craf-T Products
Expression sticker: Wordsworth
Other: Ivory and tan cardstocks, metal
    rim tags, green ribbon, paper flowers

Using Decorating Chalks

The colors of spring are reflected on the sweet faces of my sons and in the soft colors of the silhouette-cut velveteen. Enhancing the fabric paper with decorating chalks pulls in more colors from this delightful photo. The enhancer (a liquid easily applied over chalked areas with the sponge applicator) lets you deepen the colors to add shade and shadow as desired. More chalking is evident in the background of the expression (created by masking each row with torn paper before chalking each area of color), and on the circle tags. Glue paper flowers to the circle tags and hang with ribbon from the hold-punched lower edge of the expression tag.

Velveteen Effects

a BOY'S will is the wind's will. and the thoughts of Youth are long, long thoughts.

Spring 2002

Embossing on Velveteen

Fall colors cascade all around this rust velveteen page and down into Bear Trap Canyon. Embossing a design on velveteen is fairly simple, but be sure to choose a stamp with a somewhat bold design, since highly intricate details will generally be lost in this process. To emboss, position a dry rubber stamp against the right side of the fabric, turn the stamp and the fabric over together, and firmly iron the wrong side for 10 to 15 seconds. Repeat this randomly all over the fabric as desired. Chalk the images and the title as shown. Cut out a leaf accent from the area that the photo will cover. Form freehand wire curls to help tie together the title letters and to lay a path for the journaling to take shape.

Autumn Canyon

Design and photography: Jill Miller

ADVANCED

Rust velveteen: Making Memories
Decorating chalks, eraser, Pixie and Pudgy applicators: Craf-T Products
Large maple leaf, falling leaf stamps: Mostly Animals
Autumn letters diecuts: Deluxe Cuts
Copper wire, copper brads: American Tag Company
Gold glitter gel pen: Marvy
Other: Mustard yellow cardstock, iron

Hoho Holidays

Design: Jill Miller
Photography: Carolyn Holt

ADVANCED

White velveteen: K&Company
Decorating chalks, E-Z Enhancer, Pixie and Pudgy applicators: Craf-T Products
Metal letters: Making Memories
Vellum quotes: Memories Complete
Other: White, evergreen, and red cardstocks; iron

Enhancing with Color

White velveteen offers the best platform for adding bright colors, yet the embossing not be as clearly distinguishable as on colored velveteen. Thus, once your design is embossed, add colors only to the open fields within the heat-stamped image and not over the crushed impression lines themselves. Fill in the open spaces with darker and lighter tones to bring out the image and produce dramatic results. (See "A Boy's Will," opposite, for a similar technique.) Because a large portion of the ground will be covered by your photo, you can create additional stamped images and cut these out to add more layers as desired. Silhouette-cut the interior edges of your corner designs and tuck your matted photo underneath.

Incorporating Rub-ons

A close look at this layout reveals that the design is actually very simple. The page is divided roughly into quarters. A strip of brown paper with window cuts is layered over plaid fabric. Only three sides of the left-hand photos are adhered so that diecut tags can be inserted underneath. Diagonal strips of fabric are attached with nailheads; providing a backdrop for the title and slots for the pull out invitation (which is available as a free download on www.hp.com/go/activitycenter). Rub-on phrases work well on fabrics as well as on paper and can be the perfect finishing touch to a fabric project.

Give Thanks

Design and photography: Jill Miller

BEGINNER

Sepia specialty paper: Family Archives
Pilgrim and Indian art: Hewlett-Packard
Laser-cut letters: Deluxe Designs
Nailheads: American Tag Company
Rub-on phrases: Making Memories
Other: Plaid fabric strips and scraps

Polka Dots, Plaids, Wallpaper

Jack

Design: Cary Oliver
Photography:
Shaun Austin
Photography

BEGINNER

Fabric polka dot
   paper, metal let-
   ters: K&Company
Rapid-dry trans-
   parency sheets,
   inkjet printer:
   Hewlett-Packard
Other: Black card-
   stock

Printing on Transparency Sheets

Cary's simple yet stylish scrapbook page centers on a single photo of her nephew Jack. The original color photo is on the right; on the left, various tinted photos have been printed in black and white and in sepia color conversions on photo paper and transparency sheets (which allow the red fabric to show through the light areas of the photo). When you find that one special photo, try giving it even more pizzazz by printing on all types of media.

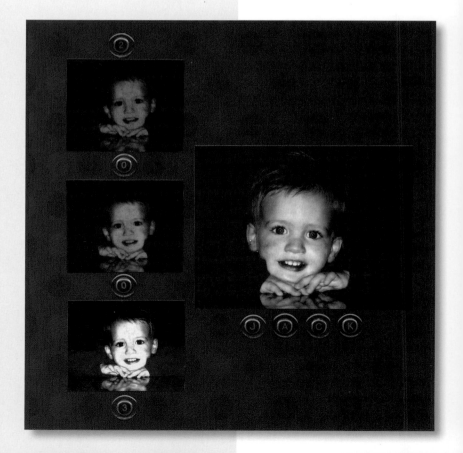

Johnny 2002

Design: Jill Miller
Photography: Beth Olsen

INTERMEDIATE

Brass hinge, mini brads,
 bookplate:
 www.foofala.com
Other: Brown cardstock,
 embossed wallpaper
 samples, gold gel pen

Hinged Journaling Flap

Old embossed wallpaper and a coordinating border combine with a metal hinge and a bookplate to offer a brand-new take on the standard scrapbook page. Try looking for new scrapbooking supplies at places other than craft and scrapbooking outlets. The materials used here are possible finds at home improvement centers, stationery shops, sign stores, or decorating showrooms. Ask your retailer for discarded wallpaper sample books and you'll have a wealth of unique scrapbooking papers at your fingertips—generally at no cost! Cut out a large border motif, mount it to cardstock, and hinge it to the page to create additional journaling space. Even more interactive page ideas are scattered throughout this book (see, for example, "Side by Side" on page 12).

CHAPTER SEVEN

Stitched Effects

No-sew scrapbookers, don't skip over this chapter! Yes, stitch effects sometimes require the sewing machine, but they can also be achieved with prestitched papers, dimensional iron-ons, paint, or a pen. Anyone can handle the simple pen stitching or prestitched paper effects that begin the chapter; even the floss whipstitch that follows is easily mastered. Next come iron-on faux-stitch appliqués both plain and painted, then we advance to edge stitching with a serger and zigzag stitching on your sewing machine. Don't despair if you're not experienced with the machine: I've kept most of the stitching simple enough even for no-sew scrapbookers.

Easy Stitch Look

Bumpkin Patch
Design: Jill Miller
Photography: Melodie Jones
BEGINNER

Pale orange and green cardstocks: Bazzill
Specialty paper: Wubie Prints
Pumpkin laser-cuts, title: Lil Davis Designs
Wire, button, small rhinestones: JewelCraft
Threads: Fibers by the Yard
Green gel pen: Marvy

Gel Pen Stitching

To make this page stand out from the ordinary cut-and-paste page, simple pen marks are added to the lettering to mimic real stitching, and crystals are added to the photo corners and the "Patch" title. Even the swirling wire that frames each photo is easy to manipulate. Just loosely curl a long length of wire around a pen or pencil, poke the end through the cardstock, and tape it to the back of the page. Gently pull the curls into swirls and twist and turn the wire to create the desired flow around each photo. To turn the first letter "P" into a "B" in the title, cut small curving strip of orange cardstock and attach it to the bottom of the "P." Cut a green tag, add journaling and threads, and tuck it behind the top photo.

Prestitched Paper

Pastels are great backgrounds for black-and-white photos, and the stitched designs in these papers make them even more delightful. Follow the stitching to create unique swirling edges. Use a bit of photo watercolor paint to bring out a touch of color in the photos, and challenge yourself to write a story that uses as many of these fun silver accents as possible.

Make a Wish

Design and photography: Jill Miller

BEGINNER

Prestitched mulberry papers:
  Creative Imaginations
3-D birthday accents:
  Westrim
Embossed seals: Hot Off The
  Press
Lettering stickers:
  Stampendous
Silver gel pen: Marvy
Spiral clip, silver paper:
  Making Memories
Photo watercolors, brush:
  Savoir-Faire
Other: Booties, knit cap

Cherish Sarah and Charlotte

Design and photography: Jill Miller

ADVANCED

Embroidered napkin: Target
Specialty embossed cardstock: Club Scrap
White rub-on words: Making Memories
Silk flowers, embroidery floss: Michaels
Small tag, wire clips, vellum

Napkin Pocket

A simple embroidered napkin serves as the material for a fabric triangle pocket. To diminish bulk, first cut the napkin in half along the diagonal. Fold the bottom left and top right point over to the lower right corner to create a square. With glue dots, secure to embossed cardstock as shown. Cut the second piece of napkin in half and fold point to point to create a triangle. Whipstitch the long side of the triangle and, with foam tape, secure the bottom and side edges over the napkin square to create a pocket. Cut small cardstock photo mats and adhere a fabric rectangle cut from leftover scraps of napkin. Add photos, printed journaling, and flowers, and wrap all with threads as shown. Burnish on words as desired to finish.

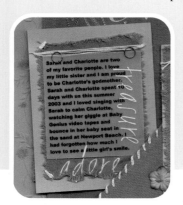

Live, Laugh, Love

Design: Jill Miller
Photography: David Thornell

INTERMEDIATE

Rose iron-on stitch effects appliqué: Delta Crafts
Opalite iridescent inks: Tsukineko
Label stickers: Pebbles Inc.
Other: Black cardstock, sponge or facial tissues, white pencil

Faux Appliqué

This stark white iron-on rose contrasts nicely against the inked-sponged black background. To create this simple frame, use a white pencil on black cardstock to mark the rose outline; remove the rose and cut along the marked line. Sponge on iridescent inks as shown. Replace the rose and iron it on, following manufacturer's directions. Trim the lower edge and frame opening as shown. Add photos and label stickers to finish this strong yet delicate no-fuss frame.

Iron-on Stitch Effects

Embroidery Look Motif

Soft black-and-white tones blend with the pale pink background and soft white accents in this piece. Even the thick gray wire words, faux-wax seal, and silver rim of the small tag have been dabbed with white opaque paint to soften the darker colors. As in "Blushing Bride" (page 8) and "Summer with Emily" (opposite), an iron-on faux stitched accent is used but not on fabric; this time an embroidered cross is ironed directly onto the cardstock background. Precut windows have been torn on two sides and the torn scraps flipped over to reveal the lighter pink on the paper's reverse, accenting the photo edges in a unique way. Mount the terrycloth to a cardstock base with spray adhesive. Secure the terrycloth base to the backside of the paper with a simple straight stitch. Fluffy white yarn with a hanging mini book adds a nice finishing touch to these tender photos.

Treasure a Miracle

Design: Jill Miller
Photography: Mars Meyer

INTERMEDIATE

Perspectives precut background: Making Memories
White shag terrycloth, white yarn: Jo-Ann Fabrics
Stitch effects iron-on: Delta
Blanco white Fiesta ink: Jacquard Products
Wire words, faux-wax seal, poem stone letter, mini book: Creative Imaginations
Other: Plain cardstock, metal rim tag, silver gel pen, small sponge or facial tissue

Painted Iron-ons

Emily's sweet expressions perfectly complement these delicate painted fabric appliqués. For the page flipper, fold a precut six-window cardstock so the openings in each row line up; trim off bottom excess. Tape a square of vellum above the middle window and another below; adhere an expression sticker to each, then wrap the entire piece with a small silk scarf and attach at the inside edges with Supertape. Trim small garlands from an iron-on sheet and heat-set on each side (follow manufacturer's directions). Print small photos onto printable silk and print journaling onto vellum (leave space in center and cut opening for photo). Adhere vellum to the left side of the cardstock base. Trim silk photos, fray the edges, and adhere to the page flipper as shown. Attach the folded panel just to the right of the journaling with a long row of Supertape and cover with silk ribbon to finish page flipper. Paint the remaining garland and trimmed bouquet as desired. With foam tape (do not heat-set or remove paper backing), adhere photos and bouquet onto cardstock base so they stand away from the page. Burnish on words and heat-set remaining florals; paint florals and burnished words (the words won't absorb the paint), and slip a panel of original photos into the top of the page flipper (fold over the top of the panel to keep the panel from falling down inside). Add a circle tag and more words to finish.

Summer with Emily
Design: Jill Miller
Photography: Mars Meyer

ADVANCED

Pink precut cardstock, white rub-on words: Making Memories
Floral bouquet iron-on stitch effects appliqué: Delta Crafts
Silk scarf, printable silk sheets: Jacquard Products
Fabric paints: Sherrill Khan: Jacquard Products
Vellum, expression stickers: Wordsworth
1/4-inch Supertape, foam tape: Therm O Web
Other: Circle tag, pink silk ribbon

Serging the Edges

Whipstitching details—all done with a serger—mimic the ironwork of the Eiffel Tower accent. Begin by covering the cardstock base with fabric and whipstitching the edges. For the folded pocket, fold a third of the money envelope up to the center and open the flap at the top as shown. Whipstitch the outside pocket top and secure the fold by whipstitching all the edges to finish. With a white gel pen, journal on strips of black cardstock, add postage stamps, insert into negative-strip holders, and place in top pocket as shown. Insert the map into the lower front pocket. Whipstitch the mat. Surround the photo with definitions blocks, add one definition to the tag, and hang from pocket as shown.

Girlfriends in Paris

Design: Jill Miller
Photography: Beth Olsen
ADVANCED

Fabric background: K&Company
Eiffel Tower laser-cut: Lil Davis Designs
Definitions blocks, small tag: www.foofala.com
Money envelope: American Tag
Large postage stamps: Stampington & Co.
Metal letter: Making Memories
Other: Plain cardstock, serger, white gel pen, black cardstock, negative-strip holder

Alli

Design and photography: Cary Oliver
INTERMEDIATE

Polka-dot wire-edged ribbon, buttons: ScrapArts
Red seed beads, small thick frame: Westrim
Letter stickers: Making Memories
$1/8$-inch Supertape: Therm O Web
Other: Black and white cardstocks, sewing machine

Machine Zigzag

Though it may seem a bit strange, you can feed paper through a sewing machine to add zigzag accents. Cary has also covered Supertape with red seed beads (press beads firmly into the tape and tap off the excess). Alli's supermodel glossy matted photo is surrounded with festive gathered ribbon. To do this, simply pull the wire along one edge of the ribbon and push gathers together until you achieve the desired effect. Hold everything in place with more Supertape on the back and adhere buttons, more photos, and journaling to finish.

Pleated Pocket

Yet another way to add fun effects to papers of all varieties is to sew a zigzag stitch or two or twenty as Cary has done with this Western-themed double-spread scrapbook page. To create a clever pleated pocket, fold a full-size sheet of paper into five rows of pleats and stitch along the bottom (to create slim pocket). Working on one pleat at a time, fold back the surrounding pleats and stitch across the top edge. When all rows have been sewn, stitch down the right and left sides to hold your pleated rows together. Experiment with a few folds on plain paper to make sure you are not sewing all your edges closed. Print your photos in black and white to complement the dark red of the papers, and adhere them to tags and paper strips that have been further accented with zigzags.

Hope for the Future

Design and photography:
Cary Oliver

INTERMEDIATE

Patterned specialty papers,
   3-D stickers, acrylic seals:
   K&Company
Walnut tags: 7gypsies
Photosmart printer: Hewlett-
   Packard
Other: Sewing machine

CHAPTER EIGHT

Ribbons and Threads

Even if you have never added fabric to your scrapbook pages, chances are you have affixed a bit of ribbon or thread to a page or two sometime. Some of the techniques here may look familiar, but be sure to take a closer look at these clever creations. You'll discover pockets made from overlapping ribbons, ribbon banners and borders, as well as mixed-up mosaics mounted on a ribbon grid (which makes a tricky technique easier to master). Photo frames and mats made with ribbons and threads, lattice backgrounds of ribbons, and a ribbon-striped background round out our celebration of these two cornerstones of scrapbooking accessories.

Summertime Girl

Design: Jill Miller
Photography: David Thornell
BEGINNER

Red polka-dot paper, green and tan
   cardstocks, heart stickers, letter
   stamps, green ink: PrintWorks
1-inch-square hole punch: Marvy
Other: Sage green organza ribbon

Ribbon Whipstitch

Dress up a simple scrapbook page with ribbon-whipstitched edges. Just hole-punch your edges and thread with ribbon. If your ribbon runs out before you finish threading all the holes, simply tape the end to the back of your page and begin a new piece where you left off.

Shipmates

Design: Jill Miller
Photographer unknown
INTERMEDIATE

Script stamp, vellum: Stampin' Up!
Red ink, sponge: Tsukineko
Diecut heart, key: Deluxe Designs
Red sheer ribbon (1 yard for 6-
   inch-square card)
Heart nailheads: American Tag Co.
Festive threads: www.thecard-
   ladies.com
Gold gel pen, black pen: Marvy
Other: Black and white cardstocks

Wrapped Ribbon Pocket

Red accents are perfect for this sweetheart card. Begin by stamping script on white cardstock and trim to fit inside a 6 x 6-inch black base. Sponge red ink through a heart diecut; add a photo to the front and a journaled vellum heart (trimmed to size) to the back. Wrap ribbon to create a photo pocket. To start, cut slits along the middle edges of the sponged heart; feed ribbon through the right slit and tape the loose end on the back. Fold ribbon at a 45-degree angle, secure in place with a nailhead, and wrap around the opposite corner and back up, placing ribbon just below first stretch of ribbon. Wrap ribbon around back and to the front just below mid-left; wrap around lower right corner, and back to mid-left, just above other stretch of ribbon. Fold ribbon over on the left, secure fold with a nailhead, tuck into left slit, and tape end on back. Add the last nailhead on bottom to finish pocket.

Border, Pocket, Banner, & Grid

Ribbon Banner

The hunt is on for clever ways to add journaling yet maintain a clean and simple scrapbooking style. To aid us here, a vellum-mounted laser-cut Easter egg opens to reveal journaling hidden under each swirl. This fancy egg and coordinating title would be lost without the ribbon banner that anchors it to the page. Add white shadows along the egg swirls but don't sweat the white shadows of the title. These come with the purple words right off the store shelves, making this page a simple and fun layout.

Easter Egg Hunt

Design and photography: Jill Miller
BEGINNER

Laser cut title, egg accents: Li'l Davis Designs
Clear and purple vellum: K&Company
White paint pen: Marvy
Other: Pink, lilac, white and mint cardstocks; gold-edged white ribbon

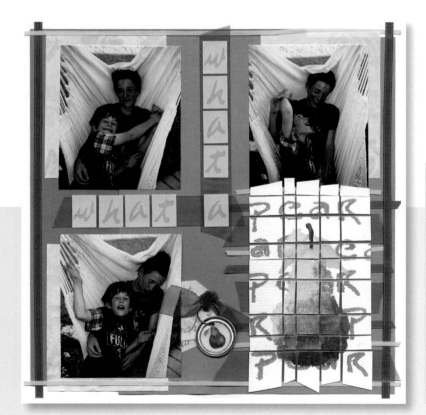

What a Pear

Design and photography: Jill Miller
INTERMEDIATE

Mulberry cardstock: Sanook
Tag book diecuts: Sizzix: Ellison
Puffy pear sticker: Amscan
Lettering stickers, pear stencil: Club Scrap
Shimmering paints, stipple brush: Radiant Pearls
Other: Sage green cardstock, green pen, organza and satin ribbons in assorted widths, circle tag

Gridded Layout

Random mosaics can be a little tricky to piece together after you've made all your cuts, so using ribbons of various widths helps simplify the process. Cut your stenciled art into rows and columns of varying widths and lengths, then mount each row onto a ribbon of similar width. Once all rows have been adhered to their corresponding ribbons, align each row so the grid lines in each column match up, then adhere the mosaic in place with small glue dots placed underneath the ribbon, and trim each edge as desired.

Ribbon and Thread Border

Rather than seek to color-correct the distinctly blue cast of these photos, Shawne choose to embrace it and cast the entire page in pale blue and pinks (to match the babies' blushing pink complexions). To define the main photo yet keep it from over-powering the page, she framed it with sheer ribbon and outlined the frame with threads. For the title, she followed the simple instructions that came with her wire jig to create the girls' names and held them in place with brads, just as she did with the threads. Ribbon edges frame the remaining photos and visually balance the page.

Piper and Carly

Design and photography:
Shawne Osterman

INTERMEDIATE

White cardstock, printed vellum:
  NRN Designs
Pastel pink and blue threads, rib-
  bon: EK Success
Jig, silver wire: Artistic Wire
Mini brads, blue brads: JewelCraft
Heart clips: Making Memories

Jennelynn Oliver

Design: Cary Oliver
Photographer unknown
BEGINNER
Lace fabric: Jo-Ann
  Fabrics
Silver nailheads,
  corners, charm:
  American Tag
  Company
³/₄-inch Peel-n-
stick Supertape:
  Therm O Web
Powder blue and
  white satin rib-
  bons: Offray
Other: Powder blue
  cardstock, spray
  adhesive, glue or
  glue dots

Lace and Ribbon Setting

Every inch of this page is covered with fabric. A gener-ous coating of spray adhesive holds the lace to the card-stock; metal corners and nail-heads secure it further and add interest. To create the ribbon framed photo, adhere a 4x6-inch photo on 5x7-inch cardstock mat, then cover cardstock edges with Supertape. Next, wrap blue, then white, then blue ribbons around the photo over the tape as shown. To form the mitered corners, fold the ribbon at a 90-degree angle onto itself; add a dab of glue or a mini glue dot to secure.
Be sure to allow a generous amount of extra length at the beginning and end of each ribbon row so that you can tie a large bow with a hanging charm.

Freeform Mat Wrapping

A simple white frame is transformed into a forceful mat with broad swipes of earth-tone inks (applied with baby wipes) and color-coordinated thread and ribbon wrapping, all inspired by the preprinted specialty paper. The random arrangement of ribbon and threads echoes the abandon of the photos themselves. Try a loose, freeform style on your next scrapbook page and watch for dynamic results.

Butte Gardens

Design: Jill Miller
Photography: Sarah South
BEGINNER

Mat-board precut frame:
  Michaels
Specialty paper: Creative
  Imaginations
Kaleidacolor earth-tone inks:
  Tsukineko
Green organza ribbon, earth-tone
  threads, red cording:
  www.thecardladies.com
Label stickers: K&Company
Labeling title: Dymo
Other: Red cardstock, baby wipes

M and P Turn
One and Three

Design and photography: Shawne Osterman
BEGINNER

Pink checked paper, paper ribbon stickers:
  PrintWorks
Tag template: Hot Off The Press
Creative Lettering bridal font: Creating
  Keepsakes CD
Other: Fine lace ribbon, rosebud trim

Lace Overlay

Shawne's adorable daughters have their birthdays almost back to back, so this one special occasion is very special indeed. Though the girls are wearing fancy dresses, the photos reveal an informal setting—a very common circumstance for many family scrapbookers. Often, undesirable details cannot be eliminated out. That's where creative cropping comes in! Notice how the lace overlay hides these portions of these images without crowding out the little girls. The series of vertical lines created with the ribbon also helps anchor each photo and tag and divides the page into two distinct but complementary sections. Even if your ribbons vary in texture or width, unify them under a single color palate and you'll love your mixed-up masterpiece.

Oh, Phoebe Pearl, Queen of all Dogs in the Universe, we like to say! Emily picked you out, and she couldn't have done better. You never have managed to get the "sit," "roll over," and "up" commands right. I'm not sure why we still laugh with hilarity each time you try so hard ... and get it so wrong. You love going to school with us in the car each day, jumping on the girls' bed in the morning to wake them up - but I think you love cheese most of all :) I'm not so sure you loved the matching ponytails you and Em have in this picture, but I sure do. You sure picked a winner, Emily!

Queen Phoebe

Design: Melissa Smith for HP Scrapbooking
Photography: Melissa Smith
INTERMEDIATE

Printed ribbon-board back-ground, pawprint paper, letters, words: PSX
Transparency sheet (for journaling): Hewlett-Packard
Scrapbooking software (for text printing on photos): HP Creative Scrapbook Assistant
Glossy accents, black ink: Ranger
Other: Red, gold, and brown cardstocks; wide red ribbon; plain wrapping tape; ribbon slide; heart-topped pins

Faux Ribbon Board

Old-fashioned ribbon boards make great backgrounds for tucking in little treasures and photos. This ribbon-board paper comes straight off the store shelves; just a few slits cut along the ribbon edges give the illusion of dimension. The red ribbon features another easy special effect: print your text on a draft sheet of paper, securely attach your ribbon over the print, and run the draft through your printer again to print directly onto the ribbon. Remember, the tighter the weave of the ribbon, the less your ink will bleed. Be sure to affix your ribbon firmly with double-stick tape under the ribbon and plain wrapping tape over the raw edges so the ribbon doesn't get caught up in the printer feed.

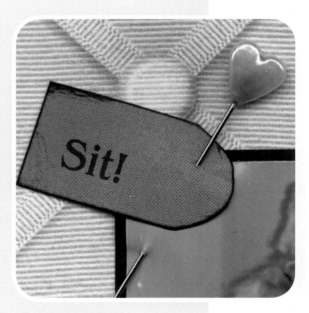

Ribbon Stripes

These photos of my sons Daniel and John David are some of my very favorites. I love their expressions of joy and the streaked sunlight coming through the wood slats of our small back porch. I choose to play off the visuals of those slats with a striped ribbon background. To create the ribbon background, wrap alternating ribbons over a cardstock base and secure the ends on the back. Cut 1/2-inch strips of black cardstock and secure over all base edges to create a page frame. Sponge turquoise ink over three small metal panels and stencil expressions with permanent ink. Mat the panels, journal the edges, and adhere over ribbon as shown. Sponge-paint the metal strip and add lettering stickers, then adhere photos and title to the page to finish.

Brothers

Design and photography: Jill Miller

INTERMEDIATE

Gold metal sheets: American Art Clay
   Company
Turquoise and black StazOn inks: Tsukineko
Sponge daubers: Tsukineko
Japanese stencils: Lasting Impressions
Lettering stickers: ChYops
Gold gel pen: Marvy
Other: Black cardstock, sheer white gold-
   edged ribbon, dark teal satin-edged ribbon

Blue-Eyed Beauties

Design and photography:
Shawne Osterman

INTERMEDIATE

Blue velveteen paper:
   K&Company
Square mini brads, lettering
   stickers: Making Memories
Blue chalk: Craf-T Products
Other: Black and white
   cardstocks, white organza
   ribbon, small blue silk
   flowers, plain wrapping
   tape, glue dots

Ribbon Lattice

Believe it or not, you don't need a ruler to make a ribbon lattice background—no measuring required. (Note that this technique works best with a square page.) All you need is a long scrap of paper (any color) trimmed to the width of the space you want to maintain *between* each row of ribbon. Then, working from the center diagonal out, wrap one length of ribbon, tape the ribbon on the back of the page, place your paper "spacer" next to the first ribbon, and attach the next diagonal row. Continue working in both directions, adding the mini brads at each intersection to keep everything firmly in place. The journaling panel also hides the many glue dots that are holding those little blue flowers and leaves in place.

CHAPTER NINE

Silk Flowers and Foliage

Ready-made silk and paper flowers and foliage are so much fun to collect and so easy to use. Since I love using flowers in my layouts, this is one of my favorite chapters in the book! I'll introduce you to interesting techniques using scrapbooking programs, paints, pastes, and embossing and antiquing mediums. You'll also see quick and clever uses for florals and foliage of all types and textures. Duplicate the advanced techniques if you wish, or just note the easy applications of Mother Nature's art replicas and adapt them to fit your own scrapbook pages.

Rose Petals and Lilacs

Digital Layering

This scrapbook page began as a pure digital page, shown below, created with a scrapbooking software program. The digital page can then be shared via email and/or printed as often as desired for special themed albums. But try printing the page in layers, then trim the prints as desired and piece them onto a larger scrapbook page. That's the time to pull out all those fabric elements, as you'll see here. The ribbon and rose petals help blend the printed elements into the page and add wonderful dimension and texture. If you like this approach, take comfort in the knowledge that this digital scrapbooking program is designed for the absolute beginner, includes a flash demo with text that provides all the instruction necessary to create a beginner-level page, and comes with a complete set of software hints.

Springtime in Paris

Design: Jill Miller for HP Scrapbooking
Photography: HP Creative Scrapbook Assistant

INTERMEDIATE

Specialty papers: Cloud 9 Designs
Scrapbooking software: HP Creative
  Scrapbook Assistant
3-D stickers: K&Company
Other: Silk rose petals, sheer ribbon,
  fabric bag

Scattered Petals

Collage specialty papers are a perfect backdrop for formal photos surrounded by a jumble of rose petals and leaves. Torn vellum mutes the background so the details stand out. Strong glue dots hold the florals to the page, while dabs of modeling paste echo the plaster statue in the photo. If you're reluctant to use the paste, just compose your page without it, but be sure to add the gold sparkle of the rose nailheads for a finished look as well as a sturdy anchor for your journaled vellum strip.

Rose Beauty

Design: Jill Miller
Photography: Shawne Osterman
INTERMEDIATE

Collage specialty paper, peach-tone vellum: Autumn Leaves
Modeling paste, palette knife: Savoir-Faire
Rose nailheads: American Tag Company
Other: Pink cardstock, pink/yellow rose petals, leaves, glue dots

Piciotto 2002

Design and photography: Jill Miller
INTERMEDIATE

Specialty papers, vellum, embossed lilac stickers: K&Company
Tag templates: Hot Off The Press
Pink gel pen: Marvy
Other: Individual silk lilac blossoms, pale yellow ribbon, craft knife

Layered Tags

Our dog Piciotto loves to lie near the flowerbeds in our backyard, so surrounding his photo with flowers is very appropriate. Construction is easy with this classic peel-and-stick scrapbook page. The layered tags add an element of surprise but these are also easy to create.

Trace three graduated sizes of tags onto a second sheet of specialty paper and cut out a window on the smallest tag (use a Post-it Note as a guide). Line the bottom of two tags with stickers and silhouette-cut as shown. Since only one sticker sheet is used to create this page, you can splurge a bit by adding beautiful silk lilac blossoms.

Echoing Floral Motifs

Brothers and Best Friends

Design and photography:
Jill Miller

INTERMEDIATE

Printed and white vellum,
   white cardstock: NRN
   Designs
Light green envelopes, spi-
   ral clips: Stampington
Journaling label tool: Dymo
   Labeler
Blossom panorama photo:
   Creative Imaginations
Other: White silk blossoms,
   mini glue dots

My three sons are reluctant to have their picture taken together, so these photos are very special to me. I was especially lucky to get them all wearing similar colored shirts and standing under these lovely blossom trees. Naturally I had to use the same light olive and white silk blossoms when creating this page. Simply feed the stems through the button clasp of each envelope and secure with mini glue dots. To further enhance the delicate white in the photo, I created embossed journaling with my Dymo labeler. Trim vellum into 1/8-inch strips and feed through the labeler just as you would the tape. If you make a mistake, just start over!

Petite whites, Tulips, and Daisy Chains

Little Girls

Design: Jill Miller
Photography: Robyn Dellamura

ADVANCED

VersaMagic spring green, green, and rose chalk-finish inks: Tsukineko

Iron-on tulip decals: Delta

Printed transparency: Artistic Expressions

Other: White and spring green cardstocks, pink organza ribbon, slide mounts, black permanent ink pen

Floral Decals

My niece Sally looks lovely against the backdrop of pink tulips perched on bright green stems. Accenting a page with silk tulips is fine for shadowboxes but I didn't want the added bulk, so I used iron-on decals. Here they are heat-set on preprinted transparency; follow the manufacturer's directions carefully and press only on the flowers themselves (don't touch the transparency directly with the iron). To create the pastel background, press the inkpads randomly against white cardstock. Repeat with the slide mounts. Adhere the photo beneath the transparency and add ribbon as shown.

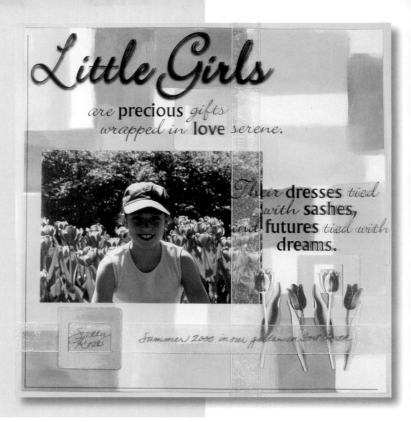

Hannah

Design: Jill Miller for HP Scrapbooking
Photography: Rebecca Bliss

INTERMEDIATE

Scrapbooking software: HP Creative Scrapbook Assistant
Daisy chain trim: Carolace
Other: White cardstock

Digital Collage

Nibbling on an infant's neck is one of the simple joys of parenthood. Remember to take a photo of their giggles so you can look back and laugh anytime you wish. To create this large dimensional page with a letter-size printer, first create a quick digital page, then print only your photos and journaling blocks by deleting your backgrounds. After printing, use the "undo" command to restore your backgrounds and delete your photos and journaling blocks to print just the backgrounds. Restore your photos and journaling blocks and save your page as a jpeg file (so you can e-mail your digital page to friends and family). Trim the prints and arrange all printed elements in layers on a larger white cardstock base to create this dimensional page. Adhere a row of daisy-chain trim down the page to visually anchor the photo to the page. (See "Springtime in Paris" on page 58 for more digital-photo inspiration.)

Silk Foliage

Leaf Collage

In Cary's photo of her hidden treasure—her little kitten, Baxter—real ferns dominate the scene; hence silk ferns make the perfect accent for her page. Each fern leaf is held in place with glue dots, and a strip of vellum anchors the many layers. Consider using many varieties of leaves under a paper banner for your next seasonal or outdoor-themed scrapbook layout.

Hidden Treasure

Design and photography: Cary Oliver

BEGINNER

Specialty paper: Paper Adventures

Black lettering stickers, wire word: Creative Imaginations

Other: Black cardstock, white vellum, silk fern leaves, glue dots

Old-fashioned Christmas

Design: Jill Miller

Photography: John LaBella

BEGINNER

Red berry stickers: PrintWorks

Sepia-conversion software: HP Creative Scrapbook Assistant

Vintage photo card and frame: *Vintage Scrapbooks,* Watson-Guptill Publications

Other: Blue cardstock, silk holly leaves

Vintage Holiday Looks

Holly leaves and berries are one of the most recognizable holiday symbols, so why not adorn your pages with these versions? Using stickers instead of silk berries eliminates bulk yet still lends a punch of color to your page. Victorian photo cards and frames are perfectly suited to heritage photos. You might also want to consider turning your current photos into sepia-toned images using simple scrapbooking software for a vintage look and classic appeal.

Sally L. Gull

1949

Glitter Accents

I love this photo of my mom sweetly smiling at the camera all dressed up in bows and braids. The soft grays of the photo are balanced by the pale pastels and beige background. Charming sentiment stickers have been applied to small vellum tags. Glitter accents highlight the skeleton leaves and the dragonflies cut from the printed vellum background and combine with the delicate lilac blossoms to surround my mom's natural beauty with nature's own elegance.

Beauty in Braids

Design: Jill Miller

Photographer unknown

INTERMEDIATE

Specialty printed and plain vellums: Autumn Leaves
Expression stickers: My Sentiments Exactly
Skeleton leaves: JudiKins
Tag diecut: Sizzix: Ellison
Glitter glue: Ranger
Other: Ivory and pastel purple cardstocks, silk lilac blossoms

CHAPTER TEN

Paper Flowers and Foliage

Paper flowers and foliage offer more options for scrapbookers than their silkier versions because they are not as bulky (some are even completely flat) and most are acid free. If in doubt, be sure to spray your flowers and foliage with a de-acidification spray before adhering them on your pages. In this chapter we will scrap with ready-made paper flowers and foliage, and I will also show you how to layer, emboss, and dimensionalize printed floral designs and foliage; use shimmering floral stickers; and create your own sparkling flowers and foliage as well as dimensional vellum bouquets.

Colors in Quadrants

Greeting Card Grid

I love receiving Christmas cards from dear friends and family. This Christmas card was especially sweet since it was hand-made, so I wanted to save Sophia's thoughtful gift on a scrapbook page. The alphabet embossed cardstock worked perfectly because I was able to cut all the letters for the title from underneath the card. I also cut each poinsettia in quarters in order to layer the sections inside the raised grid of the paper, which also allows the card to open. The silver ornaments and dimensional title add just the right amount of sparkle too.

Friends in Red

Design: Jill Miller
Photography:
Sophia Trujillo
BEGINNER
Alphabet embossed white
    cardstock: Scrap Ease
Paper poinsettias: Sanook
    Paper Company
Metal ornaments: Making
    Memories
Silver gel pen: Marvy

Special Places

Design and photography: Jill Miller
BEGINNER

Specialty paper; glitter floral, butterfly,
   and lettering stickers: K&Company
Crystal Blush, black, and olive inks:
   Tsukineko
Label maker: Dymo
Black diamond diecuts: wwwthecard-
   ladies.com
Striped ribbon: Me & My Big Ideas
Other: Facial tissues, silver wire

Colorblocking

The pale blush colors of the floral stickers are picked up in the colors that accent the folds of the specialty paper and the black diamond diecuts. Cells are created by folding the paper into sections, then olive green and black inks are dabbed inside them using facial tissues. This technique yields a colorblocked background with just one piece of paper.

My Beauty

Design: Jill Miller for HP Scrapbooking
Photography: Jill Miller
INTERMEDIATE

Printed floral art, watercolor quadrant
   art: Jill Miller for HP Scrapbooking
Laser cut title: www.sarahheidtpho-
   tocrafts.com
Purple and blue inks: Tsukineko
Tag template: Hot Off The Press
Other: Purple cardstock, embroidery
   floss, buttons, white silk daisies,
   foam tape, baby wipe, craft knife

Watercolor Features

Charlotte's natural beauty is complemented by simple watercolor daisies that I painted myself. This art is a free download from HP's scrapbooking website, along with the watercolor background needed for the tag. To make this page, download and print two copies of the daisy art and one of the watercolor background. Cut out a number of individual petals from the second print, adhere them with foam tape over the matching petal on the first print, and cut out the tag from the watercolor download. If you like, you can also blue the background of the print by dabbing the ink on edges with a baby wipe.

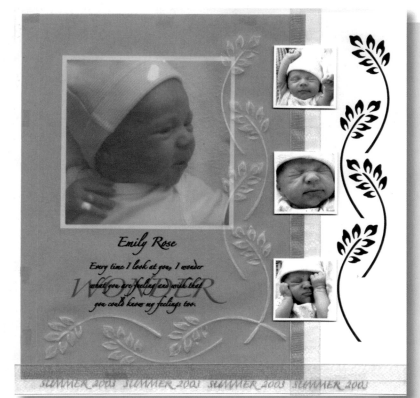

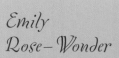

Embossed Designs

An easy dry-embossing technique creates the raised white leaves on the pink vellum in this pretty pastel page. The printed black leaves on the far right mirror the design, which is created by gently tracing each area onto vellum with a stylus. Place an old mouse pad under the vellum and printed paper design to cushion the stylus as you gently press the vellum along the lines of the design. Once you've embossed both the side and bottom of the pink vellum, turn the vellum over and piece together your page. Print "WONDER" on the pink cardstock and print the journaling on the vellum (print a rough draft on plain paper first for precision placement of text). You can also print directly onto the pink ribbon (see "Queen Phoebe," page 56, for details).

Emily Rose—Wonder

Design: Jill Miller for HP Scrapbooking
Photography: Jill Miller
INTERMEDIATE

Two printed copies of HP genealogy embossing patterns: HP Scrapbooking (free download)
Pastel pink vellum: Autumn Leaves
Other: White cardstock, pink cardstock (behind photo), embossing stylus or dried-up ballpoint pen, old mouse pad, pink organza ribbon

Autumn Smiles

Design and photography: Jill Miller
ADVANCED

Clip art leaves: HP Creative Scrapbook Assistant
Specialty paper, ivory cardstocks: K&Company
Other: Buttons, cotton twine

Clip Art Accents

The Liquid Amber trees (a type common in southern California) that grace this beautiful stretch of road near our home are especially beautiful in fall, so this scrapbook page needed fall leaf accents everywhere. To create the leaves, open your scrapbooking software, drag a single leaf onto your workspace, and duplicate as often as desired. With each copy, alter the opacity, rotation, and size, then layer each leaf as desired. Click on Add Text and type in "Autumn" in a large font size and dark color. Repeat for the second part of the quote (shown in yellow) and set color, font style, and size. Continue adding text boxes to layer text next to digital photos (rotate text from Edit menu) and print on ivory cardstock. Tear edges of all elements and adhere to page alongside buttons and string as shown.

Punched Leaves

Each morning I come upon this bend on Fairmont Boulevard as I take the kids to school, so the picturesque drive is a tradition for our family that deserves a scrapbook page (even though the kids might rather stay home!). Once again, I've used fall leaves as cascading accents but this time the leaves have been punched and covered with gold leaf flakes. The edges of the printed quote have also been brushed with glue and gilded with gold flakes. I enlarged and intensified the colors of the smaller photo to play up the highlights and show greater detail. This step is easy with just about any photo editing software. See your software owner's manual for precise instructions using the "brightness/contrast" and "image size" menu functions.

Welcome Tradition
Design and photography:
Jill Miller

ADVANCED

Specialty cardstock: Club Scrap
Large oak leaf punch: Marvy
Gold leaf flakes, adhesive: Amy Gold Leaf
Printed quote: Karen Foster
Vellum expression sticker: Wordsworth
Other: Metal hinges, mini brads

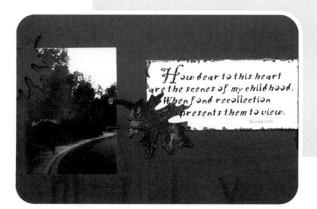

Ribbon Roses

Cary's great aunt Helen was a free spirit whose sense of fun is captured in this scrapbook page. To add more dimension to the 3-D stickers, Cary created ribbon cabbage roses by gathering one edge of a length of ribbon and securing it with a large glue dot. Small green leaves cut from the stiff green fabric paper are also held in place with glue dots. Stickers hide all these unsightly dots, and everything gets a dramatic swirl of clear glitter. To make space for extensive journaling, Cary created a paper-fabric flap, held closed by a Velcro dot hidden between the layers of ribbon roses as seen in the detail.

Helen

Design and photography: Cary Oliver
INTERMEDIATE

Specialty paper, colored stiff fabric papers, 3-D glitter, floral and lettering stickers: K&Company
Fine clear glitter glue: Ranger
Large glue dots: Therm O Web
Other: White cardstock, pink grosgrain ribbon, needle and thread, Velcro dot

Floral Tags

Design: Chantele Jacobs
BEGINNER

Paper flowers: Making Memories
Specialty papers, cardstock: Hot Off The Press
Tags: American Tag Company
Other: Buttons; ribbons; pin; blue, yellow, and brown ink; sewing machine (optional)

Button Flowers

The paper flowers in these two tags are sweet additions that give the tags great dimension. To add even more 3-D effects, both the flower petals and the tags (especially the blue crumpled one) have been brushed with inks of a slightly darker hue. Finishing details such as the zigzag stitching, pins, buttons, and ribbons reflect a great deal of love and care for the recipient of these thoughtful gifts.

On April 11, 1942, Army Chaplain Captain Wertz united in holy matrimony

Harrietta Sims and 2nd Lt. Hal Randolph

at Camp Robinson Little Rock Arkansas

Grow old along with me! The best is yet to be, the last of life, for which the first was made.

Mrs Crema Schuller was the Matron of Honor and Lt. Raleigh was Best Man. He and Hal had been best friends since their college days at North Carolina State, thru ROTC and served in the US Army together.

RANDOLPH

Randolf Wedding

Design: Cary Oliver
Photographer unknown

ADVANCED

Pastel green, blue, and white vellums: DMD Industries
Watercolor markers: Marvy
Specialty paper, vellum: K&Company
Silver frames (from vellum tags): Making Memories
Silver lettering stickers: PrintWorks
Silver square accents: Scrapyard 329
Water brush pen (or cotton swabs): Yasimoto

Vellum Calla Lilies

These gorgeous calla lilies were made with plain pastel green and white vellums, watercolor marker, and water. To begin, tear rough shapes from the vellum and moisten the edges with water from the water brush (or use wet cotton swabs). Shape vellum into flowers and leaves while wet by gently tugging on the edges and using your fingers to mold the vellum. Twist the ends of the flowers and leaves. Color the back of the vellum with watercolor markers and follow with a wet brush or cotton swab to blend as desired. The vellum will harden and retain its shape when dry. Remove vellum from two metal tags to use as frames for small photos as shown.

Although traditional quilting has been around for centuries, quilting techniques for your photos are new to most scrapbookers. This chapter will introduce you to easy quilted scrapbook pages created with faux-fabric papers using both vintage fabric scans and country quilt patterns. We also visit some advanced techniques using quilting software and puffy printed fabrics. Creative details with rainbow stitching, 3D accents, and frilly, furry fabric frames are also in store in this off-beat introduction to quilting techniques for your photos.

Easy Paper Quilt Patterns

Ian at Oak Glen
Design and photography: Jill Miller
BEGINNER
Faux-fabric backgrounds: Vintage Workshop, HP Creative Scrapbook Assistant
5 x 7 thick premade photo mat: Michaels
Other: White cardstock, tracing paper (for printing), glue stick

Vintage Fabric on Paper

Vintage fabric can be elusive and pricey, so printed papers of vintage fabric scans are a great alternate for pages with an antique touch. The backgrounds are available in the HP scrapbooking software, and are easily resized to make the quadrant-blocked background. After printing this background on tracing paper, tear all four sides and adhere strips to the edges of a white cardstock base. Cover photo mat with glue stick and adhere smaller torn strips. If desired, type journaling in four text boxes using software and rotate each line to form a frame around the photo mat. (Be sure to print on the cardstock base *before* adhering torn papers to the edges.)

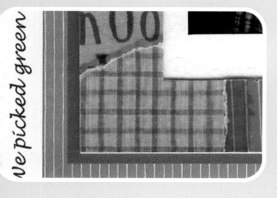

Country Quilt Squares

Three simple words, "Bless This Child," evoke strong emotions for Shawne. Inspired by this sweet expression, Shawne cut small squares of quilt-printed paper from beneath the photos to anchor her little vellum journaled tags. Torn strips of vellum have been printed with the title and also serve to cover the darker areas of the photos so they don't detract from her child's joyful smile.

Bless This Child

Design and photography: Shawne Osterman
BEGINNER
Preprinted country quilt paper: Provo Craft
Metal vellum square tags: Making Memories
Other: White cardstock, clear vellum, foam tape

Love Patchwork

Design: Elizabeth Ruuska for HP Scrapbooking
Photography: Elizabeth Ruuska
INTERMEDIATE
Iron-on Transfer sheets: HP Scrapbooking
Patterned paper: Laura Ashley: EK Success
"O" die cut: Paige alphabet: QuicKutz
Small tags: American Tag
Chalk finish ink: Rouge: ColorBox
Other: Pink cardstock, calico fabric, jump rings, safety pins, iron, ironing board

Patchwork Effect

Patchwork-style scrapbooking is a wonderful way to incorporate fabric-printed photos and faux-fabric backgrounds in your albums. This soft style replicates quilting blocks with geometric shapes and repeated patterns, made more quiltlike with the use of mini photo blocks. Elizabeth simply printed her photos on transfer sheets and then heat-set them onto calico fabric. For more about iron-on transfer sheets, see Chapter 12, "Printing and Painting on Fabric."

Quilted Memories with Software

Log Cabin

Using the Custom Quilt Label Kit, download and install the free Log Cabin expansion pack from the HP website. Launch the software and drag and drop backgrounds, images, clip art, phrases, and borders into the Log Cabin pattern as desired. Run a test print on plain paper before printing directly onto fabric sheets. Run fabric sheets through printer face down, with settings on plain paper and best quality. Remove the paper backing from the sheets. For the quilted effect, use a cheater stitch (a small decorative stitch) to bind fabric sheets to batting and backing at each grid line on the pattern before mounting the fabric sheets. Secure the print to the photo mat with fabric glue or glue dots to finish.

Priceless
Design: Deb Jungkind for HP Quilting
Photography: Hewlett-Packard
BEGINNER

Custom Quilt Label Kit: Hewlett-Packard
Free photo block expansion pack: HP Quilting
Square precut photo mat: Michaels
Other: Blue checked fabric, printable fabric sheets, batting, sewing machine, fabric glue or glue dots

Four-Patch

Using the Custom Quilt Label Kit, download and install the free Four Patch expansion pack from the hp website. Launch the software and drag and drop backgrounds, images, clip art, and borders into the Nine Patch Collage pattern as desired. Run a test print and then print on fabric sheets. Remove the backing, and cheater stitch as in "Priceless," above. Mount the finished piece on the photo mat with fabric glue or glue dots. Add embellishments to photos and rhinestones on grid lines and mount all on fabric-covered base.

Korrie and Morgan
Design: Deb Jungkind for HP Quilting
Photography: Dave McIntyre
INTERMEDIATE

Custom Quilt Label Kit: Hewlett-Packard
Free photo block expansion pack: HP Quilting
Precut pink photo mat, pink floral ribbon, beaded ribbon: Michaels
Other: Large square illustration board, printed pale pink fabric (to cover base), frilly pink trim, batting, printable fabric sheets, white feather, small rhinestones, sewing machine, fabric glue or glue dots

Nine-Patch

Using the Custom Quilt Label Kit, download and install the free Nine Patch expansion pack from the HP website. Launch the software and drag and drop backgrounds, images, clip art, phrases, and borders into the Nine Patch pattern as desired. Run a test print and then print on fabric sheets. Remove the backing, and cheater stitch as in "Priceless," opposite. Mount the finished piece on the photo mat with fabric glue or glue dots. Add embellishments and a printed vellum title and mount all on fabric-covered base.

Amy's First Love

Design: Deb Jungkind for HP Quilting
Photography: Hewlett-Packard
ADVANCED
Custom Quilt Label Kit: Hewlett-Packard
Free photo block expansion pack: HP Quilting
Precut photo mat: Michaels
3-D glitter floral stickers, printed vellum: K&Company
Other: Vintage Victorian floral scroll fabric, large white square illustration board, printable fabric sheets, batting, sewing machine

Greece

Design: Deb Jungkind for HP Quilting
Photography: Deb Jungkind
ADVANCED
Custom Quilt Label Kit: Hewlett-Packard
Precut photo mat: Aaron Brothers
Rainbow thread: www.thecardladies.com
Other: Cardstock, printable fabric sheets, batting, sewing machine, fabric glue, large needle

Machine-Embroidered Border

Using the Custom Quilt Label Kit, download and install the free Nine Patch expansion pack from the HP website. Launch the software and drag and drop images and borders into the Nine Patch pattern as desired. Run a test print, print on fabric sheets, and remove the backing, as in "Priceless," opposite. Adhere the Nine Patch fabric onto colored cardstock with fabric glue and run glue lines along grid lines. Thread a large needle with rainbow threads and stitch from corner to corner and all grid lines as shown, knotting on back. Press the threads into the fabric glue to keep them taunt against the fabric. Mount the finished piece on the photo mat. Mount additional photos under the small circles and map to finish.

GREECE

For many of us, our love of painting may have been ignited as early as kindergarten. This chapter introduces you to fabric paints, which may be a new medium to some of you and are not nearly as intimidating as some people fear. We'll be painting on cardstock and vellum as well as on canvas. We'll also explore special printing techniques using all kinds of printable fabrics, including a brief discussion on creating your own printable fabric. If you fall in love with painting or printing on fabric, you can find lots of great information and inspiration online at www.hp.com/go/scrapbooking, www.hp.com/go/quilting, www.deltacrafts.com, www.marvy.com, and www.jacquardproducts.com.

Printing on Canvas and Cotton

Distressed Edges

In this double-page spread, the right photo looks woven and has some pretty distressed edges. That's because it was printed on coated canvas and the edges were heavily sanded to expose the canvas. Just run the canvas, rather than photo paper, through your printer. To play up the distressed look, I also sanded all the cut openings as well as the printed symbols and journaling. A few creases of the cardstock finish the effect.

Great Britain

Design: Jill Miller
Photography: Sally Coon
BEGINNER

Printable canvas: Jacquard Products
Precut gray cardstock: Making Memories
Genealogy patterns: HP Scrapbooking (free download)
Other: White cardstock, used postage stamps (from a garage sale), coarse sandpaper

Frayed Edges

Look closely and you'll see that each photo is printed on canvas with the edges picked and frayed. To create this look, score your photo edges and rip them rather than cutting cleanly with scissors. Accentuate the fray by bending your canvas edges, then sand the crease. Pick apart the loose threads as desired. Add a touch of whimsy over your photos with strips of transparency that has been edged with a copper paint pen, inscribed, and secured with a mini brad. A finishing touch with the copper pen on the lettering stickers and strands of cotton twine add to the ragtag effect.

Parts Perfect

Design and photography: Jill Miller
BEGINNER

Printable canvas: Jacquard Products
Faux canvas specialty paper: The Paper Loft
Transparency sheet: Hewlett-Packard
Lettering stickers: Creative Imaginations
Metal letters: K&Company
Copper paint pen, black permanent pen: Marvy
Other: Cotton twine, mini brads, coarse sandpaper

American Beauty

Design: Jill Miller
Photography: Sarah South
INTERMEDIATE

Specialty papers, accents: Hot Off The Press
Brown chalk: Craf-T Products
White Brilliance ink: Tsukineko
Other: Navy blue cardstock, strips of cotton fabric

Journaled Fabric Strips

Charlotte loves parades and fireworks so her Fourth of July smile is surrounded with patriotic colors and accents, paired with soft beiges. For the journaled fabric strips, type the text and print a draft on paper. Firmly affix the fabric and tag over the journaling and run through the printer again to print directly on the materials. Rip the fabric into strips and fray the edges. "Age" the white fabric with brown chalk and layer over and under the page elements as shown. (For more ideas on printing on fabric or ribbon, look forward to more inspiration or look backward to Chapter 8, "Ribbons and Threads.")

Fabric Paints with Paper, Vellum, and Canvas

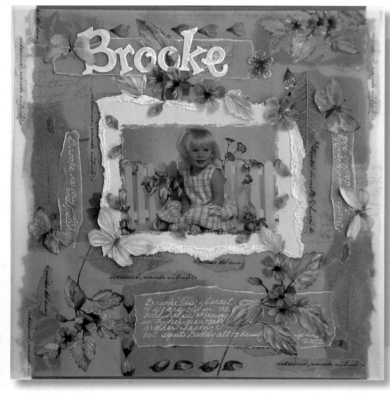

Brooke

Design: Jill Miller
Photography: Jeff Thornell
BEGINNER

Liquid Appliqué paint, gel pen: Marvy
Preprinted and plain purple vellums:
   Autumn Leaves
Letter diecuts: Sizzix: Ellison
Silver skeleton leave: JudiKins
Other: White and purple cardstocks,
   small paintbrush, craft knife, heat gun
   (optional)

Puff Paint Highlights

The subtle highlights of preprinted vellum are easily accented with heat-sensitive puff paint. The effect is dramatic texture with pops of white shine. Begin by squeezing out a *thin* line of paint over the highlights. Smooth out each line with a paintbrush and puff up paint with a heat gun (or let dry overnight). Cut out the center butterfly and flowers, journal torn vellum strips, and adhere the photo (this one was printed directly onto lilac cardstock) and accents on vellum. Add the title and accent the edges of the title and photo with paint for even more drama.

A Year of Change

Design: Jill Miller
INTERMEDIATE

Red, yellow, green, and white Liquid Appliqué paint: Marvy
Jumbo oak and birch leaf punches: Marvy
Lettering diecuts: Sizzix: Ellison
Snowflake and sunflower stencils: American Traditional Stencils
Large dragonfly diecut: www.thecardladies.com
Chalks: Craf-T Products
Other: Colored cardstocks, clear glitter, sponge, plastic plate, heat gun (optional)

Mixed Media

This four-seasons design is perfect for the first page of a "through the year" scrapbook album. Each panel is full of dimensional color thanks to fabric paint. When used on cardstock or vellum, fabric paint adds incredible texture. A mix of colors is found in the fall and spring leaves, while pure white wisps grace the dragonfly's wings. Add glitter to the wet paint on the dragonfly body and the snowflakes before puffing with heat

(or let dry overnight). For the snowflakes and sunflower, puddle paint onto a plastic plate and sponge through a stencil. Add chalk shading on the sunflower and dragonfly wings after they're heat-set, and layer all elements on cardstock mats.

Olsen

Design: Jill Miller

Photography: Beth Olsen

INTERMEDIATE

White Liquid Appliqué paint: Marvy

English rose paper, stickers: K&Company

Matte finish photo paper: Hewlett-Packard

Five 4x6-inch white mosaic grids: DieCuts with a View

Other: Gold and sage sheer ribbons, plastic plate, small paintbrush, sponge, heat gun (optional)

Accenting with White

Johnny's high-flying white hair inspired white highlights everywhere, including the photos themselves. Squeeze paint onto a plastic plate and sponge printed photos as desired. Heat-set the paint (or let dry overnight). Repeat sponging with white grids if desired. With a small paintbrush, add white fabric paint to the printed highlights of the English rose paper and heat-set. Trim the outer edges of all grids and position photos under three grids as shown. Cut away detracting grid lines and adhere all to paper (silhouette-cut the flower edges and tuck grids underneath). Finish with ribbon ties and lettering stickers.

Bundled Up

Design and photography: Jill Miller

ADVANCED

Two 12x12-inch stretched canvas blocks: Aaron Brothers

Dimensional snow, acrylic shimmer paints, iron-on stitch snowflakes, palette knife: Delta Crafts

2410 printer/copier/scanner: Hewlett-Packard

White run-on words: Making Memories

Other: Facial tissues

Dimensional Snow

Stretched canvas blocks let scrapbookers showcase their art directly on the wall, without glass! The canvas accepts paint beautifully and the dimensional snow visually extends the photo boundaries to the canvas edges. For a crystallized snow look, dab blue and white paints onto the canvas with facial tissues while the snow texture is still wet; let dry. For the poster print, enlarge a small photo on an HP color copier by selecting "poster" and "2 pages wide" (be sure to place longer photo edge down right side of glass). Print b&w draft first to check correct position and tiling effects, then print in color on glossy photo paper. Adhere to page, iron-on stitch snowflakes (follow manufacturer's directions), and burnish words to photos to finish.

Printing on Iron-on Transfers and Custom Fabric Sheets

Vintage-Look Transfers

Cary uses heritage photos to honor her ancestors' skills as seamstresses by accenting her fabric-printed images with zigzag stitching and hundred-year-old buttons worn by the women in the photo. To print photos on fabric, place iron-on transfer sheets into the printer's paper tray and print in Normal print-quality mode. This gives the photos a faded look and increases the amount of texture from the transfer sheet that shows through. These photos have been trimmed and stitched to actual wool fabric, as has the frayed fabric journaling block. The ribbon and stitched plaid background are actually printed designs whose fine details fool the eye even when placed behind actual fabrics!

Homespun Heritage

Design: Cary Oliver
Photographer unknown
BEGINNER

Inkjet printer, iron-on transfer sheets: Hewlett-Packard
Faux-wool weave printed paper, tags: SEI
Other: Frayed wool fabric scraps, buttons, sewing machine

Emily

Design: Melissa Smith for HP Scrapbooking
Photography: Melissa Smith
INTERMEDIATE

Iron-on transfer sheets: Hewlett-Packard
Custom button kit: Dritz
Cupid art background, printed tiles: PSX, HP Scrapbooking
Swirl foam stamp: Making Memories
UTEE clear and black pigment ink (for LOVE): Ranger Industries
Other: Brown textured paper, muslin, cotton fabric (for large photo and small buttons), pink metallic paint (for photo), colored pencils, sandpaper, heat gun, tulle, silk flowers

Canvas Texture

Emily's sweet smile takes center stage in this textural page. Iron the photo transfer onto woven canvas for an artistic touch to complement the quilted background and dimensional accents. This technique is duplicated in the charming photo buttons. Fun flowers, free art accents, tulle fabric, free cupid background art, and a stamped filigree finish this delightful design that treats us to the wonders of printing on fabrics.

Forty Years

Design: Barbara Schipplock for HP Scrapbooking
Photography: Barbara Schipplock

INTERMEDIATE

Spray adhesive: Krylon

Art letter tiles, definition and diamond background: PSX, HP Scrapbooking

Patterned paper, walnut tags, printed twill ribbon: 7gypsies

Decorative brad, blossom: Making Memories

Typewriter Key words: K&Company

Filmstrips: Rachel Greig

Brown Ink: Ranger

Ribbons: Cool Spool

Other: Brown cardstock, calico fabric

Custom-Printed Fabric

You can see the sparkle in their eyes, the laugher in their smiles, and the warmth of their embrace in Barbara's tribute page to her parents enduring love. She has surrounded her focal photo with vintage-style art and soft accents, as seen in the fabric-printed background and the walnut-stained tags. To create custom printable fabrics, cover the entire back of the fabric and adhere it to text-weight paper (or use self-adhesive sticker sheets) and run it through the printer when printing downloadable art backgrounds (or even your photos, if desired). For more details on creating printable fabric sheets, check out the websites listed at the beginning of this chapter.

INDEX